Things To Remember About Writing

WRITING

- Use chronological order to sequence events. Use logical order to sequence a description.
- Write an outline to help you organize ideas for a report.
- Use a topic sentence in cause-and-effect writing. Place the topic sentence first or last in the paragraph.
- Keep in mind the mood you want to create when you choose details to describe setting, character, or situation.
- Look for similarities and differences when you compare and contrast things.
- Use figurative language, such as similes and metaphors, to make your comparisons more interesting.
- Use facts in news stories. State opinions in letters to the editor. Base opinions on facts.
- Use words with positive or negative connotations to make your point in a description.
- Use first- or third-person point of view, depending on how much of the characters' thoughts you wish to reveal.

REVISING

- Add adverbs to your writing to tell how, when, or where.
- Use connecting words to link sentences and to make cause-and-effect relationships clear.
- Use specific nouns, verbs, and modifiers to make sentences clear.
- Remove unnecessary and misplaced modifiers.
- Combine short sentences and omit repeated words to give your paragraphs better rhythm.

SPECTRUM WRITING

CONTENTS

1997 © McGraw-Hill Learning Materials

Project Editor: Sandra Kelley
Text: Written by Ambrose J. Burfoot, Ted Bartoletta, and Victor Perpetua
    Design and Production by A Good Thing, Inc.
    Illustrated by Sally Springer, Doug Cushman, Karen Pietrobono,
    Kris Boyd, Anne Stockwell

unit 1
Writing in Sequence

Things to Remember About Writing in Sequence

Sequence tells the order of events.

Writing

- Use chronological, or time, order to sequence events.
- Use logical order to sequence a description.
- Vary a chronological sequence of events in a story by using flashbacks to tell about something that happened earlier, by telling about simultaneous actions in different places, or by foreshadowing future action.
- Use chronological or logical order in an outline to help you organize ideas for a report. Follow your outline when you write your report.

Revising

- Add adverbs to your writing to give specific information about *how*, *when*, or *where*.
- Use specific verbs to do the job of a verb-adverb combination, when possible.

Writing in chronological or logical order

Wanda Wechsler, controversial underwater painter, had a long and interesting life. If you were going to write a short biography of her, it would make sense to describe the events of her life in the sequence in which they happened. This time sequence is called **chronological order.**

A. On the lines below, number the events of Wanda Wechsler's life in chronological order.

_____ Started painting under water while in high school

_____ Moved to French Riviera to escape criticism

_____ Born in Boise, Idaho, on February 1, 1890, during unusually heavy rainstorm

_____ Became very excited when she spilled paints in the sink in nursery school

_____ Died at eight-five, rich and happy, in French villa

_____ Experimented in France with sprays, oils, acrylics

_____ Later work hailed by critics as "masterpieces of form and content"

_____ Won watercolor contest in elementary school

_____ As a baby, never wanted to get out of her bath

_____ First paintings jeered at by critics as "washed out"

Short biographies, such as those found in who's who books, the *Dictionary of American Biographies,* or obituary columns of newspapers, usually start with a sentence that includes information about why the person was important. Then they go on to tell about events in the person's life in chronological order. Wanda Wechsler's biography might begin like this.

Wanda Wechsler, the controversial underwater painter, was born in Boise, Idaho, on February 1, 1890, during an unusually heavy rainstorm. This may, in some way, have influenced her lifelong involvement with water. Her mother said that as far back as she could remember, Wanda had always loved water. "As a baby, she never wanted to get out of her bath," Mrs. Wechsler recalled.

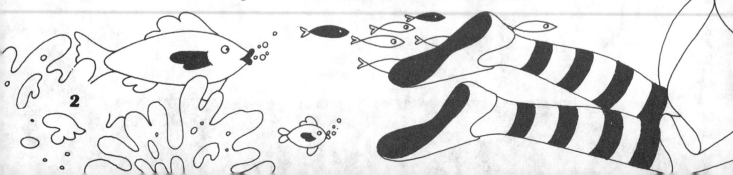

B. Refer to the paragraph at the bottom of page 2 to answer these questions.

1. Which phrase tells what Wanda Wechsler was famous as?

_____

2. Underline the sentences in the paragraph that were *not* in the list of events in part **A.** How do the sentences you underlined help show a connection between the events?

_____

C. Write up the rest of Wanda Wechsler's life, based on the events listed in part **A.** You may add more details if you wish. Try to use words and phrases that show how one event is related to another in time, such as *after that, during this time,* or *finally.* You may also wish to add phrases that show how one event influenced another, such as *because of this, since then,* or *as a result.*

_____

_____

_____

_____

_____

_____

_____

_____

_____

_____

_____

For some kinds of writing, such as biographies and directions, it makes sense to use chronological order to organize your material. Other kinds of writing can be organized in **logical order.** Suppose you wanted to describe Wanda Wechsler's painting pictured below. You might start by stating your general impression of it and then go on to tell in more detail what you see. You could describe it from top to bottom, from left to right, from large forms to small forms, or in some other such logical order.

D. Refer to the picture above to do the activities below.

1. Write a title for the painting in the space at the bottom of the frame.
2. Write a description of the painting for a catalog of Wanda Wechsler's major works. Start with an overall impression, then go on to describe the main features of the painting in an order that seems logical to you.

_____

_____

_____

_____

_____

_____

_____

4

E. Read the list of topics below. Put an *L* in front of the topics that might best be described in logical order and a *C* in front of the topics that could be described in chronological order.

_____ a stage set you painted   _____ your favorite recipe

_____ a day's trip   _____ wallpaper you designed

_____ the plot of a story   _____ your house or apartment

_____ a new outfit you bought   _____ how spiders weave webs

_____ how the tiger got stripes   _____ the gym decorated for a dance

F. Choose one of the topics in part **E.** List below the main things you will want to say about it. Then number them in logical or chronological order.

_____

_____

_____

_____

_____

_____

_____

_____

Write On

Choose one of the following.

1. Write up the topic you chose for part **F,** using the sequence you planned. Add details and transition words (like *first, next, on the top,* or *to the left.*)
2. What are your ambitions in life? Pretend that you have achieved one of your goals, and write a fictional autobiography in chronological order for the *Dictionary of American Biographies.* Think of everything you needed to do or sacrifice to reach your goal. Be imaginative. Give yourself an interesting life.

You can sequence events by using chronological, or time, order. You can sequence a description by using some kind of logical order.

Varying the sequence of events

Most stories are told from the beginning to the end in a fairly straightforward chronological progression. However, to achieve certain effects, there are several ways a storyteller can vary the sequence of events.

One way is to start the story somewhere near the middle or the end and then show earlier events in what is called a **flashback.** Read this selection.

Hurtling through space, Captain Corcoran shifted moodily in his seat, then released the restraining buckle at his waist and floated slowly out of his chair toward the control panel. He selected his favorite tape, "The Midnight Rose," and propelled himself to the center of the cabin, trying to put all thoughts of earth and home out of his mind. As the music began, he started to dance—very slowly, since sudden movements could send him crashing into the walls. He was like a diver in slow motion or a dolphin in a small tank, gracefully stretching his body, expertly gliding along the wall without ever touching it.

As he turned a slow somersault, he found himself thinking of his pole vaulting. He had always felt that gravity was some sort of enemy restraining him, holding him back, keeping him from flying. It had been exhilarating to propel himself over that bar the first time, to be free of gravity, if only for a split second. After his first jump, he had sat on the grass and thought for a long time. What if he could really get away from gravity and could float? Corcoran bumped softly against the wall. The music had stopped, but he wasn't aware just when.

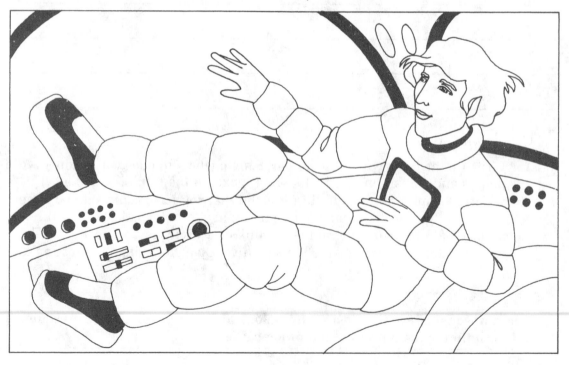

A. Think about how you might convert the scene you just read into a movie.

1. Where would the movie scene start?

_____

2. What scene would you cut to for the flashback?

_____

3. What does the flashback reveal about Captain Corcoran?

_____

B. Suppose you were going to start a story using a flashback. Circle one of the characters below and think of a present-time situation you could put him or her in that might require an explanation. Then think of a time your character could "flash back" to, or remember, that would explain something about the present.

a gossip columnist   a private detective   a comic-book illustrator
a stunt flyer   a blind musician   a fortuneteller

Present time situation: _____

_____

Flashback to: _____

_____

Another way an author can depart from a strictly chronological order is to report on **simultaneous actions,** two events happening at the same time in two different places. Read this selection.

Streaking through space in a silvery ship, concealed by the tail of a comet, the Earth Raiders have been able to approach our fragile planet undetected and are preparing to deal it a vital blow.

At this moment, on a high mountain peak, Colleen MacGregor turns her telescope to focus on Saturn.

C. Suppose that the passage above began a comic strip called "The Earth Raiders." Answer the questions below.

1. What do you think Colleen would discover in the comic strip panels that follow this introduction?

_____

_____

2. What effect is an author able to create by reporting on simultaneous action?

_____

_____

D. Below is a phrase to begin the second paragraph of a story. Think about what could be happening in the first paragraph that might create some anxiety in our minds about what was going on at the ranch. Then fill in your descriptions of two simultaneous actions on the lines provided.

_____

_____

_____

_____

Meanwhile, back at the ranch, _____

_____

_____

_____

Sometimes authors give hints about something that is going to happen. Usually, the author shares these hints with the reader while the characters in the story are unaware of them or don't realize their importance. The use of clues about future events is called **foreshadowing.** Read this selection.

A faint but distinct whirring sound woke Harriet. "I must have been dreaming," she mused. Glancing at her watch, she realized with alarm that she had dozed off on the beach and that she would be late for supper. She got up, stretched, shook out her towel, and pulled her sweatshirt over her head. She had just started up the slope leading to the beach house when she stepped on something sticky. She leaned over and pulled a light green substance off her bare foot. "Gum!" she thought in disgust. "Who on earth would have left a wad of gum out here?"

E. Think about how the story above might continue.

1. What two things in the story would you expect to have explained as you read further?

_____

2. If this story were a movie, think of something the camera could show next that Harriet would be unaware of. What would it be?

_____

_____

_____

F. Suppose you were making a movie in which one of the following dangers was in store for the main character. How would you foreshadow the danger?

a robbery   a visit of a creature from outer space   a shark

_____

_____

_____

_____

_____

 Choose one of the following.

1. Write a short story using the flashback situation you thought of in part **B.**
2. Continue the "Meanwhile, back at the ranch" story you started in part **D** using more scenes of simultaneous action.
3. Continue the story you started in part **F.** How does the main character escape from danger? Or is it too late?

A chronological sequence of events in a story can be varied by using flashbacks to tell about something that happened earlier, by telling about simultaneous actions in different places, or by foreshadowing future action.

Writing and following an outline

An **outline** is a valuable writing tool, especially when you are organizing material for a report. If you are attempting to cover too much in your report, your outline will help you see this. Your outline can also help you identify areas that you must research more thoroughly; it will point out gaps or weak links in your report.

First you must determine the sequence of your outline. Certain topics lend themselves to certain kinds of sequence—for example, a history or biography can be neatly arranged in chronological order.

A. The topics below belong to an outline for "The History of Comics." Use chronological order to rearrange the main heads and subheads into a clear order. Write the topics next to the correct numbers and letters below.

> "Mutt and Jeff" first daily in 1907
> New comics combine humor with satire
> The earliest comics
> "Superman" and "Prince Valiant" follow in thirties
> Adventure strips of the thirties
> Some old comics continue in the seventies
> "Hogan's Alley" first comic in 1895
> "Dick Tracy" started in 1931
> Modern comics

The History of Comics

I. _____

   A. _____

   B. _____

II. _____

   A. _____

   B. _____

III. _____

   A. _____

   B. _____

Other kinds of outlines can be organized in some kind of logical order. In any outline, you must be certain that the main heads are all parallel and that each subhead is placed under the appropriate main head.

B. Suppose you are writing a report about modern American music. Which of the following would be appropriate, parallel main heads? Write the Roman numerals I, II, III, and IV in front of your choices.

_____ The Beatles _____ French ballads _____ Early Egyptian music

_____ Folk music _____ Rock music _____ Scott Joplin

_____ Show music _____ Piano music _____ Country/Western music

C. Once the main heads are arranged, you can fill in the subheads and the sub-subheads, or details, below them. Fill in the subheads and details below in the logical spaces in the outline. (Hint: Look for three parallel subheads first, and then fill in the details that go with each subhead.)

Woody Guthrie   Western prairie songs   Imported folk songs
Mexican songs   Famous folk singers   Songs native to America
Joan Baez   New England sea chanteys   Pete Seeger
English ballads   Black American spirituals   West Indian calypso

I. Folk Music

   A. _____

      1. _____

      2. _____

      3. _____

   B. _____

      1. _____

      2. _____

      3. _____

   C. _____

      1. _____

      2. _____

      3. _____

Be sure your report follows the order of your outline, unless you make a decision to reorganize it. Use each main head as the main idea of a paragraph, and use the subheads as details. Don't leave out any subheads, and don't write facts in one paragraph that belong in a different section.

D. Below are part of the outline on American folk music and a paragraph based on it. Read them, and answer the questions that follow.

    C.   Songs native to America
       1.   Western prairie songs
       2.   New England sea chanteys
       3.   Black American spirituals

People sang as they worked, and many American folk songs developed out of work situations. Cowhands sang songs like "The Chisholm Trail" and "Streets of Laredo" to quiet the cattle or to help fill the lonely hours on the trail. Spirituals, like "Go Down, Moses" and "Swing Low, Sweet Chariot," although religious in content, were often sung to accompany the ship loading and plantation work done by slaves and later free workers in the South. During the Depression years of the thirties, Woody Guthrie traveled among migrant workers. His songs, like "This Land Is Your Land," told of the beauty of the American country.

1.   Which is the main idea of the paragraph?

_____

2.   Which subhead was left out?

_____

3.   Underline the sentences that fit under a different section, according to the outline in part **C.**

_____

4.   Under which part of the outline do these sentences belong?

_____

The writer may decide to move these sentences or to reorganize the outline.

12

E. Choose your favorite kind of modern American music from the main heads in part **B.** Write part of an outline about your topic on the lines below. You may wish to choose musical styles, songs, or performers to outline.

My favorite music: _____

A.   _____

   1.   _____

   2.   _____

   3.   _____

F.   Now write a paragraph that follows your outline for part **E.**

_____

_____

_____

_____

_____

_____

_____

_____

Write On Choose one of the topics below or a topic that you are especially interested in. If you need to, research facts to make an outline for your topic. Sequence your outline in chronological or logical order. Then write a short report based on your outline.

My Favorite Sport (its history or famous players)
UFOs (or other strange phenomena)
A biography of a famous person
An Event That Changed History

In an outline, you use chronological or logical order to help you organize ideas for a report. Follow your outline when you write your report.

Revising

Adding adverbs

Adverbs tell how, when, where. Some adverbs are single words and some are phrases.

	How	**When**	**Where**
Adverbs	gingerly	yesterday	outside
Adverbial phrases	without a trace	on July 4th	above the clouds

A. Fill in the blanks in the sentences below with one-word adverbs or with phrases. In the parentheses after each sentence, write whether your adverb tells when, where, or how.

1. The game began ———————————. (———————)

2. She screamed ———————————. (———————)

3. Igor arrived ———————————. (———————)

4. The snow stopped ———————————. (———————)

5. The workers sang ———————————. (———————)

Well-used adverbs can make your writing more descriptive and clear. But it is easy to overuse adverbs. Inexperienced writers tend to use too many adverbs to make up for poor verb selection. Notice how one specific verb can take the place of each verb–adverb combination below.

walked slowly—strolled   spoke loudly—yelled
did very well—excelled   taught again—reviewed

B. The paragraph below contains too many adverbs. Read completely through the paragraph once and then revise it by crossing out unnecessary adverbs. You can also cross out verb–adverb (or verbal–adverb) combinations and substitute more specific verbs (or verbals).

   Paco first heard the strange noise as he was sitting easily on the sofa, lightly holding the evening newspaper in his hand. He wanted to read it carefully because he was wishing strongly to find a sale on stereo equipment. Then he heard the noise once more. He finally decided that he had better look closely, so he walked softly through the hallway until he gradually reached the bathroom. Then he stopped to listen attentively once again. No doubt about it: A scratching sound was coming regularly from the bathroom. Paco quickly decided that a bold approach would work best, so he bravely opened the door and moved directly into the bathroom.

C. On the lines below, write two more sentences about Paco. First, tell what he found in the bathroom. Then tell what he did about it. Use at least one how, one when, and one where adverb.

_____

_____

_____

_____

 Look over the papers you have written for this unit. See which ones have too many adverbs that can be replaced with specific verbs. See which ones may need more adverbs to pinpoint how, when, or where something happened. Choose one paper to revise.

Add adverbs to your writing to give specific information about how, when, or where. But don't overuse adverbs. A specific verb may often do the job of a verb–adverb combination.

Post-Test

1. Decide whether the topics below are best written in chronological or logical order. Write C for chronological or L for logical on each blank.

   _____ a. a biography

   _____ b. a description of a city

   _____ c. a description of a ball game

   _____ d. a description of the planet Jupiter

2. Choose one of the topics below. Organize your ideas about the topic in outline form on the blanks below.

   a. clothing styles   b. computers   c. team sports

   _____   _____

   _____   _____

   _____   _____

   _____   _____

3. Write a short anecdote about one of the following: your first day at a new school, a blind date, or going to a party where you don't know anyone. Start from a present-time situation, and use the flashback technique.

4. Rewrite each sentence. Replace the underlined verb-adverb combinations with specific verbs.

   a. The assembly greeted the president enthusiastically.

   _____

   b. Jean wrote a note carelessly to her homeroom teacher.

   _____

   c. Tony differed strongly with Denis over which football team was the best.

   _____

unit 2
Writing About Cause and Effect

Things to Remember When Writing About Cause and Effect

A **cause** tells why something happens. An **effect** is what happens.

Writing

- Use the topic sentence in a cause-and-effect paragraph to describe a cause with the other sentences giving effects, or to describe an effect with the other sentences giving causes.

- Place the topic sentence either first or last in the paragraph.

- Let the reader discover the cause or causes when you write a mystery. Make the crime or fearful situation your effect.

- Go from the effects you observe to their probable causes when writing about a scientific experiment.

- When you write syllogisms, begin with a generalization and then reason your way to a specific conclusion.

Revising

- Use connecting words, such as prepositions, conjunctions, and relative pronouns, to link sentences and to make cause-and-effect relationships clear.

Writing topic sentences in cause and effect paragraphs

We see **causes** and **effects** every day. Alarm clocks wake us up; rain causes us to open umbrellas; hunger causes us to eat. Much of our writing involves describing causes and effects.

One very common method of organizing paragraphs is from cause to effect. In some paragraphs the first several sentences state obvious, observable causes. The final sentence **(the topic sentence)** then describes the effect of these causes.

A. Read the following sentences, which make up the beginning of a paragraph. Think about what effect these causes will most likely have. Then underline the best topic sentence of the three choices listed below the paragraph.

> Several consecutive years of drought have made life miserable for lettuce farmers in Southern California. At the same time fertilizer prices have doubled as the cost of oil skyrocketed. Labor expenses have risen, too, as the result of union-organizing drives.

1. As a result, many farmers have decided to grow oranges instead of lettuce.
2. These rising costs are forcing farmers to think about buying more land so they can harvest larger crops.
3. It's no wonder, then, that consumers are paying more for a head of lettuce now than they did three years ago.

In other cause-and-effect paragraphs, the topic sentence gives the cause. Then several effects are listed to complete the paragraph.

B. The topic sentence is missing from the paragraph below. Read the effects and figure out the most likely cause. Then fill in the best topic sentence from those below the paragraph.

How do we know? One sure indicator is the sale of sporting goods equipment, which has been rising at the rate of 15 percent over the past five years. Sales of running shoes particularly have been so strong that factories can't keep up with the demand. Tennis, bicycling, backpacking, and soccer equipment are also selling at higher-than-ever-before levels. Members of the medical profession supply more confirmation that millions of Americans have a regular exercise program. Cardiologists, for example, are reporting for the first time since World War II a decrease in heart attack rates.

1. Americans have always been great sports enthusiasts.
2. At last Americans have begun to exercise regularly.
3. Heart disease is less of a problem now than it once was.

C. The following sentences from a cause-and-effect paragraph are scrambled. Number the sentences in the correct order. Start by identifying the topic sentence and deciding where it should go in the paragraph.

_____ By morning, Johnny felt as if he were sleeping in a cold puddle.

_____ It began when he tried to set up his tent and discovered that he didn't have a centerpole.

_____ The raw oatmeal he ended up eating for breakfast made him feel slightly sick.

_____ One night of camping was enough to turn Johnny into a nervous wreck.

_____ Although the sky was clear and starry for a while, a drenching rain soon started, pouring through the sides of his tent and soaking his sleeping bag.

_____ He thought that a hearty breakfast would make him feel better—until he tried to light his camp stove and found that it was out of gas.

_____ He solved that crisis by tying the tent to a couple of trees, but then he learned that you can never rely on the weather forecast.

D. Look back at part **C** to answer these questions.

1. Was the topic sentence in part **C** a cause or an effect?

_____

2. Did you place it first or last in the paragraph?

_____

You have seen that cause-and-effect paragraphs can be organized in several ways. The topic sentence can come first. If it states a cause, it is followed by several sentences that give effects. If it states an effect, it is followed by several sentences that give causes. When the topic sentence comes last, it usually states the effect of the causes listed in the preceding sentences.

E.   The two paragraphs below are each missing a topic sentence. Read the paragraph, adding up the causes or effects. Then fill in an appropriate topic sentence on the blank lines. In the parentheses, write whether your topic sentence is a cause or an effect.

_____

_____ (_____)

When the magician tried to make a coin disappear, several coins fell out of his sleeve. Then he tapped his top hat to make a rabbit appear. When he lifted the hat, however, there was nothing under it. As he started to leave the stage, the magician collided with the rabbit, hopping out from behind the magician's cabinet.

The day after the early peas were planted, twelve inches of snow fell on the field. Then followed two months of sunny, dry days that first melted the snow and turned the field into a mudpack, and then baked the soil and roasted the shallow roots of the pea plants. The sun kept away the fungus diseases, but it also wilted the

uppermost leaves of the plant.   _____

_____

_____ (_____)

F. Choose one of the topic sentences below and put an X next to it. Decide whether it describes a cause or an effect. If it describes a cause, list several possible effects on the blank lines. If it describes an effect, list several possible causes.

_____ It was the worst storm in several years.

_____ I never laughed so hard.

_____ Having only one bathroom can be a problem.

_____ So now we have a pet raccoon (or other pet).

_____ Of all days to oversleep, why did I pick Friday?

_____ I haven't spoken to Dana since that day.

_____

_____

_____

_____

_____

_____

Write On Choose one of the other topic sentences from part **F** to develop into a paragraph. Or, if you like, think of your own topic sentence. Decide whether to put the topic sentence first or last. Then, to complete the paragraph, add several sentences that give causes or effects.

In a cause-and-effect paragraph, the topic sentence may describe a cause with the other sentences giving effects, or it may describe an effect with the other sentences giving causes. The topic sentence may come first or last in the paragraph.

2 Writing a mystery

Mystery stories often begin with effects—a murder, a robbery, a kidnapping. Then the rest of the story tells how the cause or causes were discovered. Mysteries like these are often called **whodunits.** In a whodunit, the detective plays an important role. He or she must put the clues together to form a chain of effects and causes that lead back to the person who committed the crime.

A. Number this chain of causes and effects in the correct order to solve "The Case of the Missing Necklace."

_____ The butler was the only one with the key to Lord Lumley's room.

_____ Footprints in the dirt near the bushes were made by size 13 boots.

_____ Both a necklace and its case were taken from Lady Lumley's room.

_____ The detective then determined that the size 13 boots belonged to the chauffeur.

_____ Muddy size 13 boots were found in Lord Lumley's room.

_____ The case was found discarded in the bushes under her window.

_____ The butler claimed he lent the key to the chauffeur.

_____ However, Lord Lumley was away, and his room was locked.

The thief was _____

The most important character in a whodunit is usually the detective. The detective may be a police officer, a private detective, or someone who specializes in solving crimes. Or the detective may be an amateur—perhaps someone who poses no threat and whom people would talk to freely, or perhaps someone with special powers. Read this description of one detective.

Ponsonby looked rather fat and stupid as he slumped in his chair. But beneath the small, close-set eyes and bald head, his steel trap of a mind was racing to put the clues together. Suddenly he sat up straight and smiled, fingering his red beard. "I've got the answer, inspector," he drawled.

B. Choose a character to be your detective. Put an X next to one of the people below or write in your own idea. Then describe your detective's appearance and skills on the lines below.

_____ a former pickpocket   _____ a little old lady

_____ a girl with a photographic memory   _____ a fortuneteller

_____ A Navajo police officer   _____ a French detective

Own idea: _____

_____

_____

_____

_____

C. Choose a situation below or think up your own. Then briefly outline the plot, giving the chain of causes and effects that lead to a solution of the crime.

_____ A priceless stamp has been stolen from the post office.

_____ The governor's daughter has been kidnapped.

_____ All the cows on a ranch have been poisoned.

_____ All the residents of one apartment building have been robbed on consecutive Tuesday nights.

_____

_____

_____

_____

Another kind of mystery is a **horror story.** Read the following.

Out of the fog, the footsteps came closer. Jenny wanted to scream, but no sound came through her clenched teeth. Then, from the mists, she saw a huge, caped figure and heard its cackling laugh. As it lunged toward her, everything went black.

Horror stories create fearful situations by using things that people are afraid of— places like dark alleys, creatures like bats and vampires, events like thunderstorms.

D. Make a list of at least five things people are afraid of. Think about frightening places, creatures, and events.

_____

_____

_____

_____

_____

In a horror story, the hero/heroine is often just an ordinary person who is affected by the fearful situation. This person must find the cause and stop it.

E. Choose a hero/heroine for your horror story—perhaps it is you yourself or someone you know well. Write a short description of your hero/heroine below.

_____

_____

_____

_____

_____

F. Now choose the fearful situation—perhaps from those you listed for part **D.** Explain in a few sentences how your hero/heroine will overcome the horror.

_____

_____

_____

_____

_____

G. Write the opening for your horror story, in which your hero/heroine realizes that something is wrong.

_____

_____

_____

_____

_____

 Choose one of the following.

1. Develop your whodunit story from parts **B** and **C.** Include at least three clues that lead the detective to find the solution.
2. Write the horror story you started in part **G.** Show how the hero/heroine overcomes the fearful situation.

Mystery stories include whodunits and horror stories. In a mystery, the effect is the crime or fearful situation. The cause or causes must be discovered.

---

3 Writing about cause and effect in science

Scientists often use cause and effect in their work. In order to find causes, they sometimes set up experiments in which they use two groups (of animals, plants, and so on) and treat each group differently. Then the scientists observe the effects. If there are not too many variables—that is, if the two groups and their treatment are similar enough—the scientists can determine what caused the different effects they observed.

A. Read the following description of an experiment. On the lines below, tell whether you think Carlotta Braun's conclusion is warranted and why. Is it based on absolute proof of a cause-and-effect relationship? Or are there too many variables?

Carlotta Braun conducted an experiment with white mice to determine if there was any relationship between their weight, reward foods, and speed of learning a maze. She constructed a simple maze and tested two groups of mice—a "fat" group and a "thin" group. The "fat" mice were given a piece of cake if they correctly ran through the maze. The "thin" mice received some carrot. When her results showed that the "thin" mice learned the maze much faster than the "fat" mice, Carlotta concluded that carrots are "brain food."

B. Read the two selections that follow. Then, on the lines, write a final sentence for each. Be sure your sentence reflects the correct cause of the effects that are described in the paragraphs.

1.   How does sunlight affect plant growth? A group of students at Franklin Junior High decided to find out. One Monday morning they planted three dozen sunflower seeds in identical clay pots. They gave them exactly the same amounts of water and fertilizer. The students put twelve of the pots in a dark closet and left them there. They put twelve pots outside for just two hours a day. They put the final twelve outside for six hours a day.

   After three weeks the plants in the closet were dead. The plants receiving two hours of sunlight daily averaged 4.3 inches in height, while the ones receiving six hours of sunlight were 7.1 inches tall on the average.

_____

_____

_____

2.   Dr. Ralph Lowell received a grant from the National Foot Care Association to test his theory of foot blisters. They were caused, he believed, not by friction, but by the color of the socks or shoes worn.

   To examine this theory Dr. Lowell devised a questionnaire that he distributed to a thousand students at the state university. He asked each of these students to mail the questionnaire back to him anytime in the next year that they got blisters.

At the end of the twelve-month period he had received seventy-four reports of blisters. In every single case the student got blisters from playing a sport, going on a long hike, dancing, or taking part in some similar activity. The students got blisters while wearing white socks, brown socks, green socks, argyle socks, no socks, black shoes, red shoes, sneakers, and just about every other possible color of socks and shoes.

_____

_____

_____

The **syllogism** is a favorite device of scientists who are testing their theories. A syllogism is an argument consisting of three parts—the major premise, the minor premise, and the conclusion. The major premise states a given generalization. The minor premise states a specific situation. The conclusion follows logically from the first two parts. Here are examples of correct and faulty syllogisms.

Correct

All *A* is *B*.	All dogs are animals.
This is *A*.	This is a dog.
Therefore it is *B*.	It is an animal.

Faulty

All *A* is *B*.	All dogs are animals.
This is *B*.	This is an animal.
Therefore it is *A*.	It is a dog.

Obviously, there are other animals besides dogs.

C. Use the examples above to help you decide whether each syllogism below is correct or faulty. If it is correct, write *C* on the line. If it is faulty, write *F*.

_____ 1. All scientists use computers.
Justina Morales uses computers.
Therefore, Justina Morales is a scientist.

_____ 2. All green plants contain chlorophyll.
This plant is green.
Therefore, it contains chlorophyll.

_____ 3. Homes heated by 100 percent solar energy don't burn oil.
This is a 100 percent solar-heated home.
Therefore, it doesn't burn oil.

_____ 4. All machines produce heat.
This object is producing heat.
Therefore, it is a machine.

_____ 5. The planets in our solar system revolve around the sun.
Uranus is a planet in our solar system.
Therefore, it revolves around the sun.

_____ 6. Citrus fruits contain vitamin C.
Grapefruit is a citrus fruit.
Therefore, it contains vitamin C.

_____ 7. All squares are rectangles.
This is a rectangle.
Therefore, it is a square.

_____ 8. All water contains oxygen.
This contains oxygen.
Therefore, it is water.

D. On the lines below, construct two syllogisms of your own. Use two of the generalizations below or think of your own generalizations. Be sure your minor premise and conclusions follow logically from the generalizations.

All plants produce carbon dioxide.
All birds hatch from eggs.
All matter is composed of atoms.
All satellites revolve around planets.

Syllogism 1: _____

_____

_____

Syllogism 2: _____

_____

_____

Write On   Write a fictional account of a real scientific discovery. Choose one of the situations below or think of your own. Before you begin, decide whether your paragraph will move from cause to effect or effect to cause. Consider also whether the topic sentence should come at the beginning or end of the paragraph. Finally, be certain your sentences follow each other in a logical progression.

Two wheels are first attached to a wagon.
Someone first goes up into the air in a balloon.
Someone first makes fire.
Someone discovers that frozen water makes ice.

Most scientific writing involves cause and effect. In experiments, scientists go from the effects they observe to their probable causes. In syllogisms, scientists begin with a generalization and then reason their way to a specific conclusion.

Revising

Using connecting words to show cause and effect

Simple cause-and-effect relationships are clearest when ideas are tied together by connecting words. Read the following two groups of short sentences. Is the cause-and-effect relationship expressed clearly in each group?

1. Fran hit a long homerun. The ball crashed through the Krupsaks' picture window. Mr. Krupsak ran out of the house yelling.
2. The storm developed slowly. The Canadian cold front stalled over Lake Michigan. A temperature inversion stopped weather movements into New England.

Now read the following revisions of these sentences. Note the subordinate conjunctions, prepositions, and relative pronouns that are underlined. These are **connecting words.**

1. <u>Because</u> Fran hit a long homerun <u>that</u> crashed through the Krupsaks' picture window, Mr. Krupsak ran out of the house yelling.
2. The slowness of the storm's development was <u>due to</u> a Canadian cold front <u>that</u> stalled over Lake Michigan <u>while</u> a temperature inversion stopped weather movements into New England.

A. Rewrite the following groups of sentences as single sentences with connecting words. Try to make your sentences as varied as possible.

1. The roads were icy. Louanne lost control of the car. It skidded into a guardrail.

_____

_____

2. The oven thermometer was broken. Claude had no way to gauge the oven temperature. The cake came out as hard as a rock.

_____

_____

3. Several icebergs drifted into heavily traveled shipping zones. The Coast Guard had to tow them away.

_____

_____

4. The air pollution index was at the "dangerous" level. Several people collapsed. They had to be rushed to the hospital.

_____

_____

5. The noise level was intolerable. Arnold couldn't concentrate. He failed the test.

_____

_____

6. The winning time for the race was slow. The horses found the track thick and muddy. Rain had been falling since midnight.

_____

_____

7. The crowd pushed forward eagerly. Everyone stood on tiptoes. They were all trying to catch sight of the movie stars.

_____

_____

8. Sandy had used bits of wood, leaves, and flowers in her picture. It was the most unusual work of art in the contest. The judges awarded her first prize.

_____

_____

Write On

Look back at the "Write On" activities you have done for this unit. Have you clearly shown cause-and-effect relationships? Choose one that isn't as clear as it could be. When you find short, choppy, or unclear sentences, revise them by using connecting words.

Use connecting words, such as prepositions, conjunctions, and relative pronouns, to link sentences and to make cause-and-effect relationships clear.

1. Read these facts about muscles and exercise:

   During exercise, muscles produce lactic acid for extra energy.
   The body needs more oxygen to get rid of the lactic acid.

   a. Now think of a reason why you start breathing hard when you exercise. Write your reason as a topic sentence.

   _____

   b. Write a sentence about the effect of hard breathing.

   _____

2. Read the following paragraph. Then write a reasonable conclusion.

   During the robbery, the dog never barked. Neither the door nor the window had been forced open. The thief evidently found the jewels immediately: there were no signs of a search.

   Therefore, _____.

3. Supply the missing line in each syllogism below.

   a. All mammals nourish their young with milk.

   _____

   Therefore, the whale is a mammal.

   b. Pure water boils at 100° C.
      This water sample boils at 100° C.

   Therefore, _____

4. Write a paragraph explaining why the discovery of fire was vitally important to humanity.

unit 3

Writing Details

Things to Remember About Writing with Details

Details are small bits of information.

Writing Tips

- List all the details you can think of about your topic. Decide on your point of view and write a topic sentence. Then choose the details that support your topic sentence. Rank them in order of importance. Cross out those that give little support to the topic sentence.

- Keep in mind the mood you want to create when you choose details to describe the setting, character, or situation.

Revising Tips

- Use modifiers to make your writing clear and specific.

- Remove unnecessary modifiers and misplaced or dangling modifiers.

Choosing the important details

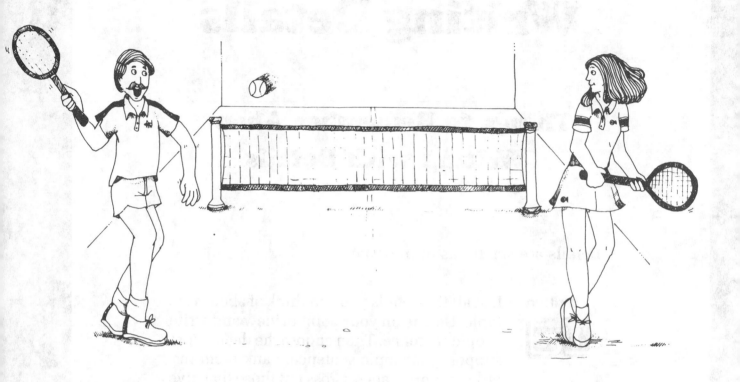

Do you see anything wrong with this picture of a tennis game? The players are using their rackets to hit the ball back and forth. But they don't seem to know that in tennis the object of the game is to hit the ball over the net.

A. Choose two of the games below. For each, state the object of the game—what you must do to score points or to win.

bowling   basketball   dominoes   football

1. _____

_____

2. _____

_____

When you are giving the rules for a game, remember that the object of the game is most important and is usually stated first. Then the necessary **details** are selected.

B. Four details about playing tennis are listed below. Choose the two that you would need to know in order to play the game. Put an X next to the necessary rules.

_____ 1. The ball must land within the boundaries of your opponent's half of the court.

_____ 2. A serve that the opponent can't touch is called an *ace*.

_____ 3. In keeping score, the term *love* means "zero."

_____ 4. After the serve, the receiver must hit the ball on the first bounce.

C. Suppose you have been hired to write nationally distributed directions for a game. Choose one of the games below, or think of a fairly simple game you know.

relay race   checkers   tic-tac-toe   volleyball

All your rules must fit on one card. Therefore you must select only the necessary details and write them in logical order. You may wish to list all the details on scrap paper first and then select and number the most important ones to write on the card below. If you feel that illustrations will help you eliminate wordy descriptions, include notes for the illustrations.

Rules for the Game of _____

Object of the game: _____

_____

Rules: _____

_____

_____

_____

_____

_____

_____

_____

Notes for illustrations: _____

_____

Choosing details is also important in paragraph or theme writing. Follow the suggestions below to select details for a paragraph.

1. List all the details you can think of about your topic.
2. Decide on your point of view and write a topic sentence.
3. Then choose the details that support your topic sentence, and rank them in order of importance.

D. On the lines below, list the details of something you have strong feelings about, such as a trip you've taken, a dream you've had, or a person you just met. List as many details as you can—at least twelve. Don't worry about their order or importance.

_____

_____

_____

_____

_____

_____

_____

_____

_____

_____

_____

E. Now decide on your point of view about the subject you chose for part **D.** Write a topic sentence that supports your viewpoint. For example, "It was the worst nightmare I've ever had" or "Although we've just met, I'm sure _____ will become one of my best friends." Write your topic sentence on the lines below.

_____

_____

_____

F. Now look back at the details you listed in part **D.** Cross out those that don't support your topic sentence, or that give it little support. Do you have five or six details left? If not, add some below.

_____

_____

_____

G. Number all your details in order of importance. Then, on the lines below, write a paragraph using your topic sentence and supporting details from parts **D, E,** and **F.**

_____

_____

_____

_____

_____

_____

_____

_____

_____

_____

_____

Write On Choose one of the subjects below, and follow the procedures you used in parts **D** through **G** to write a paragraph. Use a separate sheet of paper.

A person who makes me angry (happy, sad)
A place I (love, hate) to be
My (most, least) favorite possession

When you write the rules of a game, give the object of the game and then give the necessary, important details in logical order. When you write about a topic, choose details that support your topic sentence.

2 Using details to create a mood

The **mood** you wish to create influences the details you choose in a description.

A. Read the two paragraphs below and answer the questions that follow them.

The sun beat down on the city. Clothes stuck to people's backs. Tempers flared, and arguments could be heard on one steaming block after another.

The warming rays of the sun caressed the city streets. In the parks, people splashed in water or basked in the glowing sun. Cheery words were exchanged as people picnicked and relaxed on this beautiful summer day.

1. What are both paragraphs about?

_____

2. What mood does the first paragraph describe?

_____

3. List two details the writer chose to create the mood.

_____

4. What mood does the second paragraph describe?

_____

5. List two details the writer chose to create the mood.

_____

B. Choose two of the following situations. Write two short paragraphs for each. In the first paragraph, choose details to create a favorable mood. In the second paragraph, choose details to create an unfavorable mood.

a rainy day   eating breakfast
staying up late   dressing up in your best clothes

Topic 1: _____

Favorable: _____

_____

_____

_____

_____

Unfavorable: _____

_____

_____

_____

_____

Topic 2: _____

Favorable: _____

_____

_____

_____

_____

Unfavorable: _____

_____

_____

_____

_____

97 145

You know that the details you choose can help you create a mood. Look at the picture above. It shows someone approaching a house. When you describe the setting and the character, you can use different details, depending on the kind of story you want to write.

C. Suppose you want to write a mystery story. How would you describe the man to make him seem mysterious? Is he wearing a disguise? What might be in the bag he is carrying? What crime or horror might be awaiting him in the house? Write a short description of the character and setting on the lines below.

_____

_____

_____

_____

_____

_____

_____

D. Suppose you want to write a romance. How would you describe the man to make him seem romantic? How would you describe the setting? Is someone waiting inside the house for him? How does he feel? What's in the bag he's carrying? Write your description on the lines that follow.

_____

_____

_____

_____

_____

_____

_____

E. Suppose you want to write an adventure story. How would you describe the man to make him seem adventurous? Is he a sea captain, a spy, a deposed king? What is in his bag? What adventure awaits him in the house? Write your description on the lines below.

_____

_____

_____

_____

_____

_____

_____

_____

_____

Write On Choose one of the following to write on a separate sheet of paper. Be sure to use details to create a mood.

1. Write a story based on the character and setting you described for part **C**, part **D**, or part **E**.
2. Write about yourself. Describe a situation in which some circumstance causes your mood to change—perhaps from anger to sorrow or from fear to happiness.

> You should keep in mind the mood you want to create when you choose details to describe a setting, character, or situation. For example, you will want a different mood for a mystery than you would for a romance or an adventure story.

3 Writing details for a science-fiction story

Fact: People have flown to and landed on the moon.
Fantasy: Each person who lands on the moon is captured by moon creatures and replaced with a creature that has the same form as the human.

A **science-fiction story** is a balance between fact and fantasy. The facts come from your knowledge of people, events, and environments. The fantasy begins when you change those facts in an unusual and unexpected way.

A. Write some science-fiction ideas of your own. Use the three facts listed below, but change each one in an imaginative way to turn it from fact to fantasy.

1.   Fact: If you could travel backward in time, you might meet one of your own ancestors.

Your fantasy: _____

_____

_____

2.   Fact: In the future, more information may be stored in computers than in books.

Your fantasy: _____

_____

_____

3. Fact: The population of the world is growing faster than the production of food.

Your fantasy: _____

_____

_____

B. Now try using a fact of your own to create a fantasy.

Fact: _____

_____

Fantasy: _____

_____

_____

Choosing the right details for a science-fiction story can make both the fact and the fantasy seem convincing. Science-fiction writers use and adapt details from their own experience. That's why they sometimes create new worlds by making changes in familiar environments. Frank Herbert's *Dune* is a good example. Herbert takes a desert environment and creates an entire planet that lacks water. He can use desert nomads—the way they hunt, grow crops, dress, and travel—as models for dwellers on his planet.

C. You will now begin to create your own science-fiction world—your own planet. First, think of one outstanding feature about your planet. Perhaps its size or shape is special. Suppose the planet were a cube with two-inch sides? Suppose only six creatures lived on the cube, one on each surface? Or perhaps it is the air, the water, the plants, or the creatures of your planet that are special in some way. On the lines below, tell what is most unusual about your planet.

_____

_____

_____

_____

_____

D. Now add details about your planet. Start by brainstorming the categories below and writing two or three details for each. Think about the relationships among the categories. For example, climate will influence clothing, clothing may affect social customs, customs could change the ways families live together, and so on. Try to relate your details in a consistent way. On the last six lines, add other categories as you think of them.

Shape and size of planet: _____

_____

Terrain: _____

_____

Climate: _____

_____

Foliage: _____

_____

Appearance of creatures who live there: _____

_____

Dwellings: _____

_____

Clothes: _____

_____

Transportation: _____

_____

_____

_____

_____

_____

_____

E. When you write a science-fiction story, the world, creatures, and events you describe must be vivid enough for your readers to picture. Think of yourself on a rocket about to make a visit to your imaginary planet. Write a vivid description of what you see as you approach the planet and land there.

_____

_____

_____

_____

_____

_____

_____

_____

_____

_____

_____

_____

_____

Write On Choose one of the following.

1. Think of a problem or plot that is suggested by the planet you have created. Write a short story telling how the problem is solved.
2. Choose one of the fantasies you wrote for part **A** or part **B,** and write a story based on it.

A science-fiction story is a balance between fact and fantasy. Choosing the right details for the story can make both the fact and the fantasy seem convincing.

Revising

Using modifiers

We use **modifiers** in our writing for the same reason that we use details. Both modifiers and details make our writing specific. Modifiers—which may be adjectives, adverbs, phrases, or clauses—develop, restrict, or otherwise modify the meanings of words in sentences.

One danger in using modifiers is the tendency to use too many in trying to make our writing colorful. Consider the sentence below and its revision.

The long-distance marathon runner, exhausted from fatigue, finally collapsed past the finish line marking the end of the race, narrowly beating his equally tired opponent by slim seconds.

The marathon runner collapsed past the finish line, beating his opponent by seconds.

The underlined words in the first sentence are **redundant.** Other specific words in the sentence make them unnecessary—for example, *marathon* indicates "long distance."

A. Revise each sentence below to remove unnecessary modifiers. Keep enough modifiers to make the sentence clear and specific; strengthen nouns and verbs if necessary.

1. A dog-eared old book with the pages folded back and an old stained cover on top lay sitting on the dusty desk that hadn't been dusted in weeks.

_____

_____

2. A large, colorful crowd of gaily dressed dancers crowded onto the dance floor and danced as the loud music blared and the bright lights flashed.

_____

_____

3. The cold, freezing children huddled under the warm, cosy quilt that kept them warm in the icy, frigid room that had no heat.

_____

_____

A modifier should be placed as close as possible to the word it modifies; a **misplaced modifier** makes a sentence ambiguous. If there is no word in the sentence that a modifier can sensibly modify, we say the modifier is **dangling.** In that case, you must rewrite the sentence. Look at the examples at the top of the next page.

Misplaced: The astronomer sighted a comet through her telescope that she could not identify.

Revised: Through her telescope the astronomer sighted a comet that she could not identify.

Dangling: Unable to identify it, the comet must be unknown.

Revised: Since she was unable to identify it, the comet must be unknown.

B. Revise each sentence below to correct the misplaced or dangling modifier.

1. Coming in view of the landing sight, my fears were confirmed.

_____

2. Armed aliens crouched behind the hills, who were ready to attack at any moment.

_____

_____

3. My partner Lom decided to stay in the spaceship, who was not feeling well.

_____

_____

4. Being in Lom's pocket, I could not use the radio to get help.

_____

_____

5. I knew that someday I would tell of my adventures in space in the comfort of my own home.

_____

_____

Look over the papers you have written for this unit. Check to see that you have modifiers to make your sentences clear and specific but have not used any unnecessary modifiers. Also look for misplaced or dangling modifiers to correct. Choose one paper and revise it.

Use modifiers to make your writing clear and specific, but don't use unnecessary modifiers. Check your writing to be sure to have no misplaced or dangling modifiers.

Post-Test

1. Check the details below that would be most suitable for a report on wildlife management in a national park.

   _____ a.   Sixty miles of hiking trails are open to the public.

   _____ b.   The bear population has increased 25% since 1980.

   _____ c.   Camping is permitted from May to October.

   _____ d.   Coyotes have moved into the area.

2. Imagine a wild, windswept landscape on a dark, stormy night. Write a descriptive paragraph about it. Choose details that will create one of the following moods. Write the letter of the mood you chose next to your paragraph.
   a.   a feeling of horror
   b.   a feeling of romance
   c.   a feeling of adventure

3. Some scientists believe that space cities, built in large cylinders or spheres, will be the homes of the future. Complete the sentences below by writing two details about life in a space city.

   a.   The best thing about living in a space city is _____

   _____.

   b.   The worst thing about a space city is _____

   _____.

4. Rewrite each sentence to correct unnecessary or misplaced modifiers.
   a.   Senator Seal is the strongest champion of wildlife in Congress.

   _____

   b.   The exhausted and weary sailor told an incredible, hard-to-believe tale of survival on a liferaft in his hospital room.

   _____

   _____

unit 4
Writing Comparisons

Things to Remember About Writing Comparisons

Comparisons shows likenesses. **Contrasts** show differences.

Writing Tips

- Look for similarities when you compare. Look for differences when you contrast.
- Explain the unfamiliar by comparing it to the familiar.
- Use point-by-point order or parallel order when writing a comparison-and-contrast paragraph.
- Use figurative language such as similes, metaphors, and personification to make your comparisons more imaginative and interesting.
- Avoid mixing metaphors.
- Use analogies to clarify and add emotional appeal to an argument. Base your analogies on a comparison of a partial similarity between otherwise unlike things.

Revising Tips

- Replace dull, unnecessary adjectives with fresh adjectives and similes to make your descriptions clear and vivid.
- Form concrete modifiers by adding endings to strong nouns and verbs.

Comparing and contrasting in writing

When you **compare,** you look for similarities. Comparison of the little known to the well known can be very helpful. For example, an okapi can be compared to a giraffe, and an emu to an ostrich. If the boy in the picture had heard these comparisons, he would have been able to identify each animal.

A. Choose two of the unfamiliar things below. Write a one-sentence description in which you compare each to a better-known thing. You may use your dictionary.

dhow   blintze   serape   samisen

1. _____

_____

2. _____

_____

Comparison can also help define two similar objects more exactly. A paper clip and a staple might not seem to have that much in common until they are compared completely in form and function.

B. Choose two of the following pairs to compare. List at least three similarities between the objects in each pair.

an apple and a pear	running and walking	TV and movies
kickball and soccer	a potato and a rutabaga	tea and coffee

1. _____

_____

_____

_____

2. _____

_____

_____

_____

Contrast tells how one thing is different from another. Sometimes it is helpful to explain something by contrasting it with something it is *not*.

C. Choose two of the following pairs to contrast. Tell three ways in which they are different. For example, to contrast the sun and the moon, you could say that the earth orbits the sun while the moon orbits the earth. You could also contrast the sizes of the sun and the moon and their distances from the earth. You could note that the sun is a star and the moon is not.

tennis and badminton	the East Coast and West Coast
Chinese and Italian food	tragedy and comedy
spring and autumn	birth and death

1. _____

_____

_____

_____

2. _____

_____

_____

_____

Once you have decided on the similarities and differences of the two objects you are comparing, you are ready to develop your comparisons and contrasts into a paragraph. There are two ways of doing this: by using point-by-point order or by using parallel order. In the first, you skip back and forth between object A and object B, comparing and contrasting them one point at a time. In the second, you describe all the points of object A, then you move on to object B, describing its points in the same order.

D. Choose one pair that you compared in part **B** or contrasted in part **C.** On the lines below, write a paragraph that compares them in point-by-point order.

_____

_____

_____

_____

_____

_____

_____

E. Choose another pair from part **B** or part **C.** On the lines below, write a paragraph that compares them in parallel order.

_____

_____

_____

_____

_____

_____

_____

You can help explain something unfamiliar by comparing and contrasting it to something familiar. Sometimes, you might want to recall the familiar past and then describe how it has changed.

F. Read the following paragraph and answer the questions below.

A modern newspaper office is different from the office that many of us picture in our minds. But the difference may not be quickly grasped by a quick visit. Rows of desks and wire-service terminals still fill the office. Telephones still constantly ring. Reporters with half-empty coffee cups still scurry in a thousand different directions. But the typewriters—some of them do not even use paper! Frequently, all the typewriters in an office are electric, and their hum has become another voice in the office din. Some have special keys with special symbols. A story is typed on a piece of paper and then "read" by a computer. Other typewriters are tied into computer screens: as a story is typed, it appears on the screen and is "remembered" by the computer. The newspaper itself may be printed from "pictures" sent by the computer. A computer may play a large role in bringing your daily paper to you.

1. List two ways in which a modern newspaper office is similar to an older office.

_____

_____

2. List two ways in which a modern newspaper office is different from an older office.

_____

_____

Write a paragraph in which you compare or contrast how you look now with how you looked five years ago. Or compare and contrast your appearance now with the way you hope to look five years from now.

When you compare, you look for similarities. When you contrast, you look for differences. Comparisons and contrasts often help to explain the unfamiliar by comparing it to the familiar. A comparison-and-contrast paragraph can be in point-by-point order or parallel order.

Writing with figurative language

The Eagle

He clasps the crag with crooked hands;
Close to the sun in lonely lands,
Ringed with the azure world he stands.

The wrinkled sea beneath him crawls;
He watches from his mountain walls,
And like a thunderbolt he falls.

—Alfred, Lord Tennyson

This poem, like many others, makes its point by using **figurative language** instead of straight description. Figurative language includes **similes, metaphors,** and **personification.**

A.   Look for comparisons in the poem and answer the questions below.

1.   In a simile, two unlike things are compared by using *like* or *as.* Write a simile from the poem.

_____

2.   Tell how you think the two parts of the simile are alike.

_____

_____

3.   In personification, an animal or nonliving thing is compared to a human by giving it some human characteristic. Write an example of personification from the poem.

_____

A metaphor is different from a simile in that it does not state a comparison with the words *as* or *like*. Thus the comparison is less direct; it is harder to see that a comparison is being made. A metaphor says that one thing is the same as another. The word *metaphor* comes from the Greek word meaning "to transfer." When you use a metaphor, therefore, you transfer the meaning from one thing and apply it to the other.

B. Read these metaphors. Then answer the questions below.

The world is nothing but an endless seesaw.

—Michel de Montaigne

Friends are thermometers by which we may judge the temperature of our fortunes.

—Countess of Blessington

1. Do you think the world is like a seesaw? If so, in what way? If not, what would you compare the world to?

_____

_____

2. Do you agree with the second metaphor? If so, why? If not, what do you think friends are like?

_____

_____

C. Read each comparison below. Put an *S* in front of each simile, an *M* in front of each metaphor, and a *P* in front of each example of personification. Then, on the blank line, explain the comparison.

_____ 1. Knowledge is the food of the soul. (Plato)

_____

_____

_____ 2. Youth like summer morn, age like Winter weather (William Shakespeare)

_____

_____ 3. Money is a good servant, but a bad master. (H. G. Bohn)

_____

_____ 4. Let the rain sing you a lullaby. (Langston Hughes)

_____

_____

Figurative language is often found in poetry, but similes, metaphors, and even personification can give any descriptive writing more impact.

D. Select three of the pairs below (or choose your own pairs) and write a sentence about each pair. One of the sentences should use a simile; one, a metaphor; and one, personification.

a kite and a hawk   a friend and a bridge   a dancer and a meadow
night and a person   a skyscraper and a mountain   electricity and a stream

1. _____

_____

2. _____

_____

3. _____

_____

There is one error to guard against when using figurative language. It is **mixing metaphors.** A mixed metaphor can best be described by looking at the example below.

In every shy person, there is a hidden tiger just waiting to take flight.

Do tigers fly? This mixed metaphor can be corrected by changing the sentence in one of two ways.

In every shy person, there is a hidden tiger just waiting to spring out.
In every shy person, there is a hidden eagle just waiting to take flight.

E. Rewrite each sentence below to correct the mixed metaphor.

1. Like a ship in full sail, he confidently went about feathering his nest.

_____

2. She was an eager beaver, always ready to grab the ball and run with it.

_____

3. The clock's ticking reminded him of the beating of a drum that pounded against the shore of his brain.

_____

_____

4. Her smile was the sunshine that brightened our days and lit up the darkest nights.

_____

_____

F. Each statement below can be made more imaginative and interesting. Rewrite each, using the information in it as the basis for a figurative statement.

1. The melting snow added to the water in the river.

   _____

2. He hammered nails into the wood.

   _____

3. We were without electricity for several hours.

   _____

4. I stubbed my toe on a brick.

   _____

5. The sunset was quite colorful.

   _____

Choose one of the subjects below to write about in an imaginative way—or use the picture on this page. To give your description impact, think of at least one metaphor, one simile, and one statement using personification. Then include your figurative language in a poem or prose description of your subject.

    a city at twilight   a wild animal
    a storm   a jet plane

Figurative language includes similes, metaphors, and personification. Figurative comparisons can make descriptions more imaginative and interesting.

3 Writing analogies

captain : ship = mayor : city

The words above are called an **analogy.** The analogy can be read as a sentence: "Captain is to ship as mayor is to city." The symbol : stands for the words "is to," which express a relationship. The relationships on both sides of the equal sign must be similar. What is the relationship between a captain and a ship? The captain is the chief executive who runs the ship. What about a mayor and a city? The mayor is the chief executive who runs the city. Are the relationships on either side of the equal sign similar? Yes—so the analogy works.

bud : flower = child : _____

To complete an analogy, you must understand the relationship between the first two words. What is the relationship between a bud and a flower? A bud is small; it will develop into a flower. What will a child develop into? Fill in the word on the blank line above.

A. Now use the method above to complete the analogies below.

1. bull : cow = rooster : _____

2. elephant : mammal = ostrich : _____

3. cold : hot = young : _____

4. small : little = easy : _____

5. night : moon = day : _____

6. dish : cupboard = _____ : wallet

7. artist : painting = _____ : snapshot

8. doctor : hospital = waiter : _____

9. pond : lake = hill : _____

10. mail carrier : deliver = ballerina : _____

B. The analogies below have been started, but you must complete each to show a similar relationship.

1. man : woman = _____ : _____

2. calf : cow = _____ : _____

3. smooth : rough = _____ : _____

4. violin : orchestra = _____ : _____

5. farmer : crop = _____ : _____

6. cherry : pie = _____ : _____

7. cook : _____ = _____ : _____

In an analogy, unlike things are compared by looking for ways in which they are alike. Analogies can be used in writing to clarify a point or to make an emotional appeal. When analogies are used in writing, all four parts are not always expressed. Compare the two sentences below. The second is an analogy.

It is important to use seat belts because it has been proven that they reduce serious injuries in auto accidents.

Not wearing seat belts is like jumping off a cliff and expecting to land in a net.

C. Choose two of the items below. Write a one-sentence analogy for each.

| littering | wearing new shoes | being late |
| not doing homework | listening to rock music | going to the dentist |

1. _____

_____

2. _____

_____

A **fable** and a **parable** are both special types of analogies in story form. Both fables and parables illustrate lessons or moral truths that we can apply to our lives. In a fable, the characters are usually animals.

D. Read the short fable below and answer the questions that follow it.

A donkey was relaxing between two bales of hay. He became hungry and eyed first one bale and then the other. Both looked delicious, and the donkey could not decide which one he should eat. It was such a difficult decision for the donkey to make that he gave up and starved to death.

1. What do you think is the moral of this fable?

_____

2. How could you relate this fable to your own life?

_____

_____

_____

Now read this parable.

A man had three daughters. The two eldest never stopped telling him how much they loved him, but the youngest was silent. The father bragged about his two wonderful older daughters, but he had nothing good to say about the youngest. Then the man became ill. The two older daughters never came to see their father. They were too busy with their friends and entertainments. But the youngest daughter nursed her father and took care of him until he was better.

E. Write a moral for the parable at the bottom of page 60.

_____

_____

_____

F. Choose one of the morals below. Write a short fable or parable to illustrate it.

    Look before you leap.
    Kindness can often accomplish more than strength.
    Beware of flatterers.
    All that glitters is not gold.

_____

_____

_____

_____

_____

_____

_____

_____

_____

_____

_____

Write On

Choose a moral that has special meaning for you. Write it on another sheet of paper. Then write a fable or parable to illustrate the moral.

Analogies are comparisons based on a partial similarity between otherwise unlike things. An analogy can clarify and add emotional appeal to an argument. Parables and fables are stories which make analogies to illustrate lessons or moral truths.

Revising

Choosing adjectives

Adjectives are an important part of any writing that compares or contrasts objects. Well selected and wisely used, they add color, detail, and exactness to your writing. However, poorly chosen, overused adjectives make writing vague and cloudy instead of sharp and focused.

Read the following two sentences. In which are the adjectives better chosen?

> The big, slow boat churned lazily up the long, winding river as the still, hot sun shone down on the many resting vacationers.
>
> The huge boat churned lazily up the river as the sun shone down like a brilliant lamp on the vacationers.

The second sentence says almost everything that the first says and does it more clearly. *Huge* creates a sharper contrast with the slow, lazy images of the rest of the sentence. The simile "like a brilliant lamp" says that the sun is still, close, and intense; and it says it with an exact, concrete image.

A. Rewrite the following sentences. Eliminate unnecessary adjectives and substitute stronger ones or figurative language to make each image more concrete.

1. The long, interconnected freight train pulled gradually out of the dark, smelly, windswept freightyard and began its long, jerky journey to the faraway East Coast.

   _____

   _____

2. The manicured, lush green golf course was overrun by pushing, eager fans who wanted to see every measured inch of the swings of their favorite professional golfers.

   _____

   _____

3. The shy, quiet girl looked down at her new pink ballroom dancing shoes as the muscled, ramrod-straight young man in a perfectly tailored black tuxedo walked toward her across the polished wooden dance floor.

   _____

   _____

   _____

One way to make your descriptions fresh is to replace stale adjectives like *big*, *loud*, *old* with carefully chosen, concrete modifiers. You can form interesting modifiers by adding endings such as those below to strong nouns and verbs.

soup—soup<u>y</u> fog   thunder—thunder<u>ing</u> train   fade—fad<u>ed</u> pattern

B. Add an ending to change each word below to a modifier. Also write a noun it might modify. Think of two fresh modifiers of your own for numbers 7 and 8.

1. brood____ _____
2. grouch____ _____
3. carpet____ _____
4. howl____ _____

5. scratch____ _____
6. crack____ _____
7. _____ing _____
8. _____ed _____

C. The paragraph below is an example of writing that is colorless and dull for lack of adjectives. Rewrite it, adding fresh adjectives to create a concrete picture.

Adela reached the station early. It was big inside. Little light came into the open space. It smelled bad, and noises echoed off the ceiling. There was some linoleum on the floor. Adela sat on a bench and read a magazine as she waited for the train.

_____

_____

_____

_____

_____

_____

_____

_____

Look over the papers you have written for this unit. Check for descriptions that need more concrete images. Choose one paper, and revise it.

By replacing dull, unnecessary adjectives with fresh adjectives and similes, you can make your descriptions clear and vivid. Many concrete modifiers can be formed by adding endings to strong nouns and verbs.

Post-Test

1. Rewrite each comparison below. Make sure you unmix the metaphors.

   a. Jamie's speech was a beacon that stirred us to action.

   _____

   b. Lana's voice was a silver bell with a surprisingly sharp edge.

   _____

   c. Detective Bunsen's hawklike profile reminded me of a cheetah stalking its prey.

   _____

2. Complete these one-sentence analogies.

   a. For shy Lucy, going to a party was like _____

   _____.

   b. Max took games seriously: playing chess with him was like _____

   _____.

   c. Justin's idea of a "little" snack was like _____

   _____.

3. Write comparisons for the following:

   a. tennis ball and boomerang (simile)

   _____

   b. subway train and snake (metaphor)

   _____

   c. tree swaying in the wind and a dancer (personification)

   _____

4. Write a short fable or parable illustrating the following moral:
   As you make your bed, so shall you lie in it.

unit 5
Writing
Facts and Opinions

Things to Remember About Writing Facts and Opinions

A **fact** is an objective statement that can be tested or checked. An **opinion** is a subjective statement that expresses someone's feelings or ideas.

Writing

- Use facts that answer the questions *who, what, when, where,* and *why* in news stories. Do not include opinions unless they are in quotations. Use a lead paragraph to capture the reader's attention.

- State your opinions on controversial community issues in letters to the editor of a newspaper. Base your opinions on facts.

- Combine facts about your candidate and the issues, as well as opinions about the candidate, when you write school campaign speeches.

Revising

- Use specific nouns and verbs to make your sentences clear and accurate.

Writing a news article

News articles consist of facts that answer the *wh* questions **who, what, when, where,** and **why.**

A. Read the following news story openings. Decide which question words each opening answers and write them on the line below.

1. At noon on April 4th, Martian Scouts, velvet Venusians, and purple Plutonian plants took part in the annual Alien Day Parade.

   _____

2. Mayor Rita Greensleeves announced that she will not buy another trained cougar.

   _____

3. The town raccoon-watching committee watched into the wee hours of Sunday morning, but officials report no raccoons were sighted.

   _____

4. "I used trained monkeys to rob the night deposit box so I wouldn't get caught," the criminal sobbed as he was led away this morning.

   _____

B. Choose two of the above statements. Add made-up facts that answer the *wh* questions that the original statement leaves unanswered. For example, sentence 1 does not tell where or why the parade was held. Rewrite each statement as you add the necessary facts, but remember to include the original information. You may want to use two sentences to include all the facts.

1. _____

   _____

   _____

2. _____

   _____

   _____

A news reporter must distinguish between facts and opinions. A **statement** of fact is a statement that can be verified (checked) by observation, testing, or reference to records. Whenever possible, the reporter should tell the reader the source of his or her information. A reporter also keeps notes that list the sources of information.

A reporter should not express her or his own opinions in a news article, although the reporter might quote an opinion of a person being written about. Read these two opinions from news articles.

"The Millburn railroad station is being ruined by this ugly, disgusting graffiti and the hoodlums who put it there," Mayor LaCosta complained yesterday. "It is a blight, and it must be stopped."

Things go from bad to worse in Millburn these days. Take the railroad station, for example. It's a jungle of ugly colors and mindless scrawls. Any delinquents old enough to hold a can of spray paint must think they have the right to make their stupidity public.

The first statement could be checked by talking with Mayor LaCosta. The mayor's statement is an opinion, but it is a fact that the mayor said it. The second statement is the reporter's opinion and should not appear in a straight news story.

C. Decide whether the following statements are facts or opinions. In front of each fact, write *F*. On the line below the statement, tell how it could be checked. In front of each opinion, write *O*. On the line below, explain why it is an opinion.

_____ 1. The people of San Francisco pay more sales tax in one month than the entire population of Bolivia pays in one year.

_____

_____ 2. We pay a small fortune for professional dog-catching services, yet the city is completely overrun by increasing bands of dirty, nasty mongrels.

_____

_____ 3. Watching TV is, of course, a waste of time. But if you must waste your time this way, you might as well watch color TV—it's much better than black and white.

_____

_____ 4. Mrs. Quinn told the city council that graffiti was all right in its place. She said it would be good if the teenagers had a special place set aside for graffiti.

The opening of a news article is called a **lead.** Just as most writers work to develop interesting openings, most reporters try hard to come up with good leads for their stories. In a newspaper filled with many articles, the lead often determines whether or not a particular story will be read. Some leads are explosive, like the first example below. Others are more intriguing or thoughtful, like the second version.

Shouting "Not in our town you don't!" an angry mob stormed city hall this morning protesting a proposal to build a jail on the outskirts of town. "I got kids to think of," speaker after speaker told the applauding crowd. Amid the din of honking horns, police in riot gear held back the crowd to keep the road open.

A crowd of an estimated three hundred men, women, and children gathered outside city hall this morning to protest a proposal to build a correctional facility on the edge of the city. Speaker after speaker voiced concern for the safety of their homes and children. Helmeted police were on the scene and worked authoritatively to keep the road open and traffic moving.

The type of story often determines the type of lead. It is important that a lead give some facts and point to, or "lead" to, the rest of the story.

D. Write leads for two of the following stories. One lead should be explosive. The other lead should be more thoughtful. Include additional information to answer some *wh* questions in each lead.

1. An earthquake occurs near the site of a nuclear power plant. Officials are afraid that radioactive waste is leaking into a nearby river.
2. Four young boys are found adrift at sea after being missing for a week. They claim they were carried off to sea while playing in an old boat on the beach.
3. Two fifteen-year-old girls find one million dollars in cash in an old suitcase in a deserted garage. The police have no information about the money, and the girls will get it if it is not claimed within two months.
4. An unidentified flying object was seen in downtown Chicago by about four thousand people. Strange musical sounds and flashing patterns of lights were reported. The Air Force is investigating.

1. _____

_____

_____

_____

_____

_____

2. _____

_____

_____

_____

_____

_____

 Read the following ridiculous headlines and try to imagine the content of the news article that would follow them.

ROB JOHNSON TELLS BROTHER TO KEEP HAMSTERS OUT OF BEDROOM
CHERYL MIRANDA BUYS NEW SNEAKERS—SIZE 8C
HOWIE BERGER ASKS RACHEL BREEN TO MOVIES
MRS. BETTY RILEY CLAIMS SHE WILL BAKE CAKE FRIDAY

Write the article which goes with one of these silly headlines. Or think of an everyday occurrence that happens in your home or school and write about it in a news article. Include facts; quote an opinion; and pay special attention to the lead.

A news article contains facts that answer the questions who, what, when, where, and why. It should not include opinions—except in quotations. It is important that the lead paragraph of a news story interest the readers.

2 Writing an editorial

Most sections of a newspaper—world news, local news, business, weather—are made up of objective or factual articles. The reporter presents information that is known to be true.

Most newspapers also have an **editorial** page. On this page the editors and other writers give their opinions on events in the news. In the lead of an editorial, a writer usually reports some basic facts about the subject. The writer also provides a clue about his or her opinions on the subject.

A. Read the following editorial lead. List the fact or facts the writer reports. What is the writer's opinion?

> The general national unemployment rate has gradually yet steadily fallen for the last eighteen months. It now rests at 5.2 percent. However, the persistence of a jobless rate approaching 30 percent for inner-city youths remains one of the nation's most troubling social problems.

Fact: _____

_____

Opinion: _____

_____

B. Here is the first sentence of an editorial lead. It contains a fact.

> Today's students enjoy almost four months of vacations and holidays each year.

Write a second sentence for this lead. The second sentence should let your readers know your opinion about this subject.

_____

_____

C. Practice writing the beginning of an editorial. Choose one of the facts below to write about in the lead. Use the possible opinions to help form your own opinion or opinions. Write at least three sentences on the lines below.

Fact	Possible Opinions
In recent years there has been a 25 percent increase in school violence.	Violent students should be punished more severely. School principals should eliminate conditions that lead to violence. Violence is increasing everywhere; the government should do something.
Junior high school students are joining more competitive sports teams.	Competition is good; it helps develop people's characters. Competition is bad; it makes you dislike other people. Competition is bad because someone always has to lose.
Many eighth graders have no money to buy things that they want and need.	Eighth graders who want money should earn it. Eighth graders are not responsible enough to handle money wisely. All eighth graders should have a minimum allowance provided by their parents or guardians.

_____

_____

_____

_____

_____

How do editors choose the subjects of their editorials? They usually choose subjects that are important both to them and to the people in the community. If an issue is important, there is usually something **"at stake."** That means that depending on how the issue turns out, people in the community tend to gain or lose something—usually money, power, freedom, or security.

D. What is important to you? List at least five things about which you have a firm opinion or would write an editorial. You may want to think of issues in your community or school.

_____

_____

_____

_____

_____

Editorials are often written when there is a strong difference of opinion that is dividing a community. Important issues over which many people differ are said to be **controversial.** The writer of the editorial often hopes to persuade a majority of people to agree with either one or the other side of an issue.

E. Read these two editorial leads, each from a different newspaper. Then answer the questions below.

Teachers and other school employees should be allowed to strike for better salaries and working conditions. The right to strike is a right all Americans must have.

Teachers and other school officials have a special responsibility to their students. Teachers have no right to let their salary demands interfere with the educational development of the nation's youth.

1. What facts are these editorials discussing?

_____

2. What is the opinion of the first editorial?

_____

3. What is the opinion of the second editorial?

_____

F. Choose one of the following controversies. Write an editorial lead that expresses your opinion.

Pro	**Con**
Girls should compete against boys in organized athletics.	Girls should not compete against boys in organized athletics.
The city should cut taxes so citizens will have more money to spend on what they want.	In order to have enough money to provide services to the people, the city should not cut taxes.
The government should spend more on missiles to protect our nation.	The government should spend more on schools to provide better education.

_____

_____

_____

_____

_____

_____

When issues are controversial, emotions run at a high level. That means that unrealistic demands, threats, or predictions of disaster will sometimes appear in editorials. Most readers, however, will not be convinced or persuaded by an editorial unless it is based on facts and logical thought. An editorial must list in order the reasons that lead to an opinion.

Choose one of the controversial issues you have written or thought about in this lesson. Write an editorial that logically states the issue and your opinion.

Editorials state the opinions of editors and other writers on important, controversial community issues. An editorial should be based on facts and written logically.

lesson

3 Writing a campaign speech

It is election day in Ocean City. The town is about to elect a mayor. The polls show that two candidates are running neck and neck—each has 35 percent of the vote with 30 percent undecided. Since you are a professional speechwriter, each candidate has asked for your help. You must choose to support one, and then write the speeches that will help him or her get elected. Here's a rundown on the candidates and their qualifications.

Floyd P. Jolly	Ina O. Hartfelter
Qualifications	**Qualifications**
Has served as mayor for two terms (eight years)	Has a law degree and a degree in city planning
As a native and lifelong resident, he knows the town of Ocean City	Has been a councilwoman for four years in the city government
Has learned a great deal about management, building one clam stand into a statewide chain of seafood restaurants	Has taken an active role in improving the Ocean City school system ever since she moved to town five years ago

As a speechwriter you will also be interested in the personal qualities of the candidate you will support. Read the following lists. Think about which qualities you would emphasize if you had to introduce the candidate to a large crowd of people.

Jolly	Hartfelter
Very friendly; people like him Practical; a self-made millionaire Independent; thinks people should take care of themselves rather than let the government do it Hardworking; but always has time for fishing or a game of golf Married; enjoys holidays with his four grown children	Intelligent; has an excellent academic background and holds three advanced degrees Hardworking; usually works eighty hours a week, not including weekends Compassionate; wants the city to do more for the old and poor Single; has a few good friends; lives alone; rarely takes a vacation

A. Your first job as a speechwriter is to introduce your candidate to a large gathering of voters at a local beach. Choose a candidate. Then decide what qualities and qualifications you wish to emphasize in your introduction. Write the introduction here.

_____

_____

_____

_____

_____

_____

_____

_____

_____

_____

_____

_____

Ocean City has its share of important issues and controversies. These issues have become important in the campaign because the candidates disagree over them. Read about the issues and the opinions of the candidates.

Issue	Jolly's Opinions	Hartfelter's Opinions
Offshore oil drilling near Ocean City's beaches	Yes. The oil rigs are necessary. They will provide jobs, and the country needs oil.	No. There is no evidence that there is oil there. The rigs are loud and ugly. If oil is found, spills could ruin the beaches.
Proposed 50 percent cut of local property taxes	Yes. People deserve to keep more of their hard-earned money. Government tends to waste money anyway.	No. Ocean City needs that tax money to pay for police and fire protection, as well as to improve libraries, schools, and senior citizen centers.
Ban smoking in all city buildings	No. Smokers have rights too, and it would be too difficult to enforce.	Yes. It is unfair to make others breathe stale, smoky air.
Benson-Green Housing Renewal Site	No. The buildings are too old to save. Tear them down and put up the high rises as originally planned.	Yes. There are enough high rises already. Let residents who reconstruct old houses keep them.

B. Your candidate wants you to write some campaign "literature." It is a leaflet that will tell about the opinions of your candidate on the major issues. The leaflet will be handed to people on the street. Write the opening paragraph for this leaflet.

_____

_____

_____

_____

_____

_____

Your candidate has been asked to speak to the Chamber of Commerce. The governor will be there, and the event will be televised. Your candidate has asked you to write a great speech for the occasion.

Most good political speeches contain the right combination of factual details and well-expressed opinions. Those in office usually stress their fine records of accomplishment. Those out of office usually stress the poor record of the officeholder, the problems to be dealt with, and the solutions they propose to initiate. Political speeches often include both issues and personal details about the candidates. They appeal to the emotions as well as to the intellect. The use of repetition in a speech helps a candidate make her or his point.

C. Examine your candidate's opinions on page 76. Then plan or outline the speech your candidate will give on the lines below.

_____

_____

_____

_____

_____

_____

_____

Now write the actual speech. Stick to the outline that you wrote in part **C.** Remember to give facts as well as opinions. Repeat the important points that your candidate wants to make.

A political speech combines facts about the candidate and the issues, as well as opinions and personal qualities. Such speeches often appeal to both the intellect and the emotions.

Revising

Using specific nouns and verbs

A reporter must provide facts that are clear and accurate. One good way to do this is to use **specific nouns** in news articles, editorials, and other writing. Compare these sentences.

The guy running for city office promised a lot of things.
Mayoral candidate Floyd P. Jolly promised to cut taxes, build high-rise housing, and develop offshore oil wells.

A.   Next to each general noun below write three specific nouns.

1.   flower   _____   _____   _____

2.   drink   _____   _____   _____

3.   trash   _____   _____   _____

4.   transportation   _____   _____   _____

5.   disease   _____   _____   _____

B.   Each sentence below can be made more specific. Replace each underlined vague word with a more specific word.

1. The big red <u>building</u> on Benson Street is 150 years old. _____

2.   Those oil rigs make a loud <u>noise</u> when they drill. _____

3.   <u>They</u> work hard. _____

4.   Ms. Hartfelter is giving a speech <u>someplace</u> tonight. _____

5.   It will be about the <u>place</u> where senior citizens live. _____

Your writing will also be more exact if you choose **specific verbs.** One specific verb can often do the job of a vague verb and an adverb. Compare these sentences.

Vague: Mayor Jolly <u>went quickly</u> to Washington.

Better: Mayor Jolly <u>flew</u> to Washington.

C.   Next to each general verb that follows, write three specific verbs.

1.   walk   _____   _____   _____

2.   talk   _____   _____   _____

3. eat _____ _____ _____

D. Revise each sentence below by replacing the underlined word or words with a more specific verb.

1. Ms. Hartfelter said, "We must improve our schools!" _____

2. Mayor Jolly, who weighs over two hundred pounds, walked slowly toward the

   banquet table. _____

3. He ate quickly and talked loudly throughout the meal.

   _____ _____

4. The mayor's aides talked softly about a new poll which said Ms. Hartfelter was

   running slightly ahead of the mayor. _____

E. The sentence below is vague.

   He didn't like it when he heard it.

Revise the sentence to make it tell more. The sentence should be clear and accurate. Then use the sentence as the topic sentence of a paragraph. Add several sentences of your own, remembering to use specific nouns and verbs.

_____

_____

_____

_____

_____

_____

Look at the "Write On" exercises you have completed for this unit. Choose one to revise. Make it more accurate by using specific nouns and verbs.

Use specific nouns and verbs to make your sentences clear and accurate.

Post-Test

1. Read each sentence below. Write *N* if the sentence belongs to a news story. Write *E* if it belongs to an editorial.

   _____ a. "I think our city should give small businesses a tax break," said Mayor Roche.

   _____ b. More should be done to stop small businesses from leaving our city.

   _____ c. Scientists believe there is a small but real chance that a large asteroid may someday collide with Earth.

   _____ d. As if unemployment, pollution, and the threat of war weren't enough to worry about, now, it seems, we should be developing "anti-asteroid" missiles.

2. For each fact below, write an opinion.

   a. Teenagers spend large sums of money playing video games.

   _____

   b. Many types of math problems can be done easily on inexpensive pocket calculators.

   _____

   c. Fewer students are applying to the more expensive private colleges.

   _____

3. Write a campaign speech promoting yourself as principal-for-a-day. Mention your qualifications, personal qualities, and ideas.

4. Rewrite these sentences, using specific nouns or verbs for the underlined words.

   a. We <u>saw</u> an <u>animal</u> hiding in a tree.

   _____

   b. The writer <u>gave a prepared talk</u> about her childhood in <u>the South</u>.

   _____

unit 6

Making Your Point in Writing

Things to Remember About Making Your Point in Writing

The **purpose** of a piece of writing may be to inform, to entertain, to express feelings or opinions, or to persuade.

Writing Tips

- Create a positive or negative feeling when you write descriptions of people, places, or things by using words that have positive or negative connotations, such as *healthy* or *lazy.*

- Write better reviews by including a short summary of the work, your opinions, and your reasons for them. Then suggest whether others would enjoy it.

- Make your letters of application brief and to the point. State what the job is, how you found it, and what your qualifications are.

Revising Tips

- Combine short sentences and omit words that are repeated often to give your paragraphs better rhythm.

Using the denotation and connotation of words

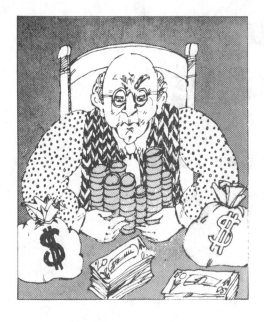 

This is the story of Ephraim Ruddy, a stingy, miserly old man.

This is the story of Ephraim Ruddy, a man who is thrifty and careful with his money.

How do you feel about Ephraim Ruddy after looking at the picture and reading the sentence on the left? Do you get the same feeling from the picture and sentence on the right? *Stingy, miserly, thrifty,* and *careful with money* all have the same basic meaning or **denotation.** But they differ in their **connotation,** the positive or negative feelings they give. Here are some other words with similar meanings but different connotations.

Positive	Negative
easygoing	lazy
ambitious	aggressive

Carefully selecting the exact words you want when writing helps you to make your point. You can create positive or negative feelings about characters in your writing, depending on the words you use to describe them.

A. Below and on the next page, you will find sentences that describe people using words with positive connotations. These words are underlined. Rewrite each sentence to give it a negative connotation.

1. Oliver takes pride in his work.

_____

2. Todd takes pride in his appearance.

_____

3. Penelope is persistent.

_____

4. Helga has a healthy appetite.

_____

A place, like a person, can be described by using positive or negative words. Read this paragraph.

I visited my cousin Alana in her cramped apartment for the first time tonight. As I entered the messy one-room apartment, I was surprised. Alana had been living there for only three weeks. Magazines and newspapers were strewn on the coffee table. Dishes were dumped in the sink. The furniture was ancient. The view from the front window was bleak. I couldn't stay very long, but I did wish Alana the best of luck.

B. Answer these questions about the paragraph above.

1. What did the writer think about the appearance of Alana's apartment?

_____

2. Underline the words in the paragraph that helped you know how the writer felt.
3. Do the words the writer used convey a positive or a negative connotation?

_____

C. Below are several sentences from the paragraph. Rewrite each sentence so that it conveys a positive connotation. An example has been done for you.

I visited my cousin Alana in her cramped apartment for the first time tonight.
I visited my cousin Alana in her cozy apartment for the first time tonight.

1. As I entered the messy one-room apartment, I was surprised.

_____

2. Magazines and newspapers were strewn on the coffee table.

_____

3. Dishes were dumped in the sink.

_____

4. The furniture was ancient.

_____

5. The view from the front window was bleak.

_____

Ad writers use words with positive connotations ("plus-loaded" words) and negative connotations ("minus-loaded" words) to try to make you buy a product. Plus-loaded words are used to describe either the product itself or how you will feel or look using the product. Minus-loaded words often describe the way you must feel or look if you aren't using the product.

D. Read the ads below. Underline the plus-loaded words and phrases. Circle the minus-loaded ones. Keep in mind that names of products can also be loaded.

a.
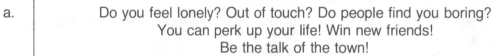

Do you feel lonely? Out of touch? Do people find you boring?
You can perk up your life! Win new friends!
Be the talk of the town!

Subscribe to **GOOD IMPRESSIONS**—
the magazine that keeps you up-to-date on
news, hit records, discos, and places to eat.

b.
Are there days when everything rubs you the wrong way?
No need to despair any longer.
Rid yourself of minor aches and pains with

SUNSHINE Liniment Ointment.

No need to rub it in. Just pour it on.
Watch your troubles float away and your shining smile return!

c.
The **SLIM-TRIM** Store offers you a golden opportunity.
The latest in slick T-shirts, stylish jeans, chic jackets,
at low, low prices to fit your budget.
Everything we sell makes you look and feel **SLIM** AND **TRIM**!!!

Come see us soon at our new store in the Cross-Country Shopping Center.

E. Below are products that need advertising. Give each one a name. Write two or three plus-loaded words you would use to describe it. Then write two or three minus-loaded words to tell how the consumer would look or feel without the product.

1. a school ring

   Name: _____

   Plus-loaded words: _____

   Minus-loaded words: _____

2. a typewriter with a circular keyboard

   Name: _____

   Plus-loaded words: _____

   Minus-loaded words: _____

3. a hand computer that gives answers in three languages

   Name: _____

   Plus-loaded words: _____

   Minus-loaded words: _____

4. a snowmaking machine

   Name: _____

   Plus-loaded words: _____

   Minus-loaded words: _____

5. a how-to book on winning contest prizes

   Name: _____

   Plus-loaded words: _____

   Minus-loaded words: _____

Write On

Choose one of the following.

1. Pick a person or place to describe. On a separate sheet of paper, write two descriptions. In one description, use words with positive connotations. Then write about the same subject using words with negative connotations.
2. Pick a product to describe. Write your description in the form of an ad. Use plus- and minus-loaded words.

When you write descriptions of people, places, or things, you can create a positive or negative feeling by using words that have positive or negative connotations.

2 Writing a review

Have you ever read a movie review that made the movie sound so exciting that you just had to see it? Have you ever read a review of a TV show that kept you from watching it?

People write reviews of movies, TV shows, books, and plays. A **review** summarizes facts about a work—characters, plot, setting, style, sets, performers, and so on. It states opinions and gives reasons for them. And it suggests whether or not other people should read or see the work.

Here is part of a review of a new book.

Donna Blakely's first book, *Echoes of the Past,* is a spine-tingling thriller. I was spellbound as I followed twenty-year-old Tess D'Aubermont on her ominous journey. Her family and friends were sure that she was crazy, but she knew she wasn't. She knew her visions were real—and she would convince everyone, if it was the last thing she ever did.

The seemingly serene setting of the small New England town contrasts with Tess's turmoil. Will she find the reasons for her visions? Is someone playing a trick on her? Or is the quiet seaside house really haunted? Does Tess really belong to the past, a past of 150 years ago?

Looking for answers to these questions—and carried along by the well-written narrative—I read *Echoes of the Past* in one sitting. I found Tess D'Aubermont a convincing character, strong willed and courageous. She stood out more than any other character in the book. In fact, I would have liked to have learned more about the other characters. Still, I applaud Donna Blakely's first book and hope that another is on its way.

A. Look back at the review to answer the following questions.

1. List three facts the reviewer gives you about the book.

_____

_____

_____

2. What does the reviewer say the book is about?

_____

_____

3. What is the reviewer's general opinion of the book? How is this opinion supported?

_____

_____

_____

4. List one thing that the reviewer does not like about the book.

_____

5. Does the reviewer seem to recommend the book to other people? Explain your answer.

_____

_____

B. Now imagine that you are a critic. You are in the audience watching the one-act play pictured below. Use the illustration to answer the questions on the next page.

1. Briefly describe the characters and setting of the play.

_____

_____

_____

2. What do you think the play is about?

_____

_____

3. What seems to be the audience's reaction to the play?

_____

4. What else would you need to include about the play if you were actually writing a review of it?

_____

_____

_____

C. Think of four books you've read, four movies you've seen, and four TV shows you've watched. List them on the lines below. Then rate them 1 to 4, starting with 1 for your favorite.

Books	**Movies**
_____	_____
_____	_____
_____	_____
_____	_____

TV Shows

_____

_____

_____

_____

D. Use the lists you made in part **C** as you follow the directions below.

1. Choose one of the movies or TV shows. Tell where and when you saw it. Or choose one of the books and tell when you read it.

_____

2. Write a short paragraph that tells what the film, TV show, or book was about. Be sure not to give away the ending.

_____

_____

_____

_____

_____

3. List several things that you liked about the movie, TV show, or book.

_____

_____

_____

4. List several things that you didn't like about the film, TV show, or book.

_____

_____

_____

_____

On a separate sheet of paper, write a review of the movie, TV show, or book you chose in part **D.** Include your short summary of the plot. You may wish to describe in more detail one scene that stands out in your mind. Then write your opinions of the show. If you chose a film or TV show, give your opinions about performers, plot, sets, costumes and dialogue. If you chose a book, discuss the characters, plot, setting and writing style. End by telling whether or not you think others would enjoy the work.

A review usually includes a short summary of the work, the reviewer's opinions and the reasons for them, and a suggestion as to whether others would enjoy it.

Writing a letter of application

Are you interested in getting a part-time job? A summer job? A weekend job? When you apply for a job, one of the first steps is to write a **letter of application.**

It is important to keep several points in mind when you write a letter of application. You should have the correct spelling of the name of the person you are writing to, as well as the correct address. You should state the job you are applying for. You should include how you found out about the job and why you think you're qualified for it. You should also decide what the point of your letter is. Are you asking for an application form, or do you wish to set up an appointment? Once you decide what the point is, get to it quickly. Your letter should not be more than a page long.

Read the sample letter below.

48 South Bend Drive
Bay Ridge, KY 40012
June 11, 19____

Ms. Louise Seiden
Manager
Paradise Bake Shop
3 Twin Oaks Shopping Center
Bay Ridge, KY 40012

Dear Ms. Seiden:

Yesterday I was in the Twin Oaks Shopping Center and saw the sign in your bake shop window for a summer assistant. I am interested in applying for the job. Although I've never worked in a bake shop, I have always helped out at home and am a fast learner. I live across the street from the shopping center and can always be at work on time. I also do not have a sweet tooth, so I wouldn't be eating as I work!

I would like to set up an appointment to introduce myself to you. I can meet with you after school hours or on weekends. My home phone number is 089-3636. Thank you for taking the time to read this letter.

Very truly yours,

Alexander Gold

Alexander Gold

A. Use the sample letter on page 90 to answer these questions.

1. Is this letter written in the form of a friendly letter or a business letter?

_____

2. How did Alexander find out about the job?

_____

3. What does Alexander feel his qualifications are for this job?

_____

_____

_____

4. What is the point of Alexander's letter?

_____

5. What other kind of information did Alexander give in his letter?

_____

Now ask yourself the question, "Why should anyone hire me?" The best way to demonstrate your qualifications is to show that you have performed similar duties in the past. This doesn't mean that you had to have a job exactly like the one you're applying for. But everyone has skills learned from past experience that can be applied to new situations.

If you have helped in your parent's home workshop, then you probably know about tools. This knowledge would be something to mention if you were applying for work in a gas station. If you have supervised a table at a bake sale, then you've shown you can handle and account for money. That would be a plus for a job as a cashier or a salesclerk. If you frequently take care of younger brothers or sisters, then you've shown responsibility in supervising youngsters, a necessary skill for a playground supervisor or a camp counselor.

Also consider your personal characteristics. Are you a hard worker? Creative or artistic? Willing to take on responsibility? Able to work with people? You should be able to prove to someone who doesn't know you that you have these characteristics.

B. On the lines below, write down qualifications and personal characteristics you have that you think would make someone want to hire you.

_____

_____

_____

_____

_____

Below is an imaginary section of classified ads from a newspaper, the *Clarion*. Read the ads. Do any of them appeal to you?

HELP WANTED at the **METRO BIKE SHOP** 21 Park Drive East Choose your own hours. Write to: Bob Hanle	**PART-TIME JOB AVAILABLE** at **House of Records** Hours: 3–6 p.m., Mon. thru Sat. We're located at 666 Main St. Make an app't with R. Gomez.
Ms. Angela Pagano needs an **Assistant Salesperson** at the Golden Arches Shoe Shop 41 Triangle Lane Part-time hours	**YOUTH** needed to help with Summer Lunch Program for kids 5–9 years old. Start at 10 a.m. Finish at 2 p.m. People's Firehouse, Inc. 212 Northside Ave. Director: Fred Dunlop
Do you like cars? Do you like to see them look brand new? The **CLEAN 'N' SHINY** Car Wash wants you! Weekends only. Send for application. 2 West End Road L. Beech, Manager	**CASHIER/PACKER** needed at H & M Supermarket 15 Knob Hill Square Saturdays and Sundays Martha Kawada, Manager
THE PIZZA PALACE needs someone to make local deliveries. H. Hertlischek 721 White Street Evening hours only.	**VERY BUSY** Veterinarian's Office needs summer receptionist to answer phones and make appointments Dr. Sarah Steiner 89 Middletown Rd. (four-day work week)
Ye Olde Ice Cream Shoppe needs reliable person to work counter. Weekends only. 33 Belt Blvd. S. Georgiades, Owner.	We need someone who can run a copying machine! **Full-time summer position** **Speedy Copy Center** 13 Highwater St. Request for application from Mr. S. Flint.
The Seascape Library has a position available. We need someone to conduct a Saturday morning story hour. 1330 Willow Lane Mr. Roy Petro, Librarian	**Goody's Card Shop** 55 Park Drive West needs someone to handle new deliveries. Send inquires to Ms. C. Wendell.

C. Choose one of the ads listed above. Imagine that you are writing a letter of application for the job. Then answer the questions below.

1. Who will you write your letter to? (If this person has a title, be sure to include it.)

2. What is the address you are writing to? (Use your own town, city, or neighborhood. Don't forget the state and zip code.)

_____

_____

3. How did you find out about this job?

_____

_____

4. List the qualifications you feel you have for this job.

_____

_____

_____

5. List personal characteristics that you feel would be good for this job.

_____

_____

_____

6. What is the point of your letter?

_____

 On a separate sheet of paper, write a letter of application for the job you chose above. Incorporate your answers to the questions in part **C.** Make sure you write a business letter. (On page 123 of the Handbook, you will find more information on writing business letters.)

Writing a letter of application is one of the first steps you usually take when applying for a job. A letter of application should be brief and to the point. It should state what the job is, how you found out about it, and what your qualifications are for the job.

Revising

Sentence and paragraph rhythm

The sentences below are from the beginning of a paragraph.

> Winters in Connecticut become unbearable. I think of summers spent in leisurely sailing. I think of summers spent in leisurely sunbathing.
>
> When winters in Connecticut become unbearable, I think of summers spent in leisurely sailing and sunbathing.

The three short sentences above have been combined into one longer, smoother sentence. In the longer sentence, some of the repeated words were eliminated and the connection between the sentences was made clearer. Too many short, choppy sentences spoil a paragraph's rhythm.

A. The sentences below continue the paragraph. Combine each group into one sentence that sounds both smooth and clear.

1. I have memories of sun-filled days. The memories get me through the slush. They also get me through the cold.

   _____

   _____

2. Winter may have pleasures for some. I find myself concentrating on ways to keep warm. I also try to keep dry.

   _____

   _____

3. I like to curl up. I read a good book. I sit in front of a fire. The fire is roaring.

   _____

   _____

4. My book is forgotten. I dream of summer. I finally feel warmth. I feel contentment. They steal over me.

   _____

   _____

B. Read the following paragraph. Rewrite it on the blank lines below, combining sentences to make the paragraph read more smoothly.

Simone stepped off the plane. She was greeted by tall tropical plants. She was greeted by sweet-smelling air. From the airport, she could see the mountains. The mountains rose in the background. They were so green. She couldn't wait to get to her room. She wanted to unpack her bags. She would take a long swim in the ocean. Simone felt so lucky. She was lucky to be home again. She was most comfortable at home. She had enjoyed her visit. She had enjoyed her grandmother. But she wouldn't trade living on this island for anything!

_____

_____

_____

_____

_____

_____

_____

_____

_____

_____

_____

_____

_____

Write On

Look over the papers you wrote for this unit. Which ones have paragraphs with choppy rhythm? Choose one paragraph and revise it on a separate sheet of paper. Remember to omit or change repetitious words and to combine sentences.

> **Your paragraphs will have better rhythm if you combine sentences and omit words that are repeated often.**

Post-Test

1. Rewrite the following sentences. Change the underlined words to words that have positive connotations.

    a. Jeffrey is so <u>nosy</u> about other people's affairs.

    _____

    b. Shawna always dresses <u>sloppily</u>.

    _____

2. Ad-writers can make any boring product sound exciting and necessary. Try writing an ad about a gadget that butters toast automatically. Pack your ad with loaded words.

3. Choose one of the jobs below. Then list some of your qualifications that could go in a letter of application for that job.

    a. junior counselor at a day camp
    b. a department store worker
    c. a part-time caretaker in a city park

    _____

    _____

4. Read the book review below. Then name two things that are wrong with the review.

    A Second Chance is a novel about a top high school basketball player named Timmy Barnes. After Timmy is crippled in a car accident, he begins a courageous struggle to walk again. I liked this story very much.

    a. _____

    b. _____

5. Revise the following paragraph so that the rhythm is improved. Combine sentences and omit unnecessary words.

    The concert started. Linda's violin string snapped. She had to go backstage to get a new string. The audience grew restless. Linda returned. The orchestra started from the beginning.

    _____

    _____

unit **7**
Point of View in Writing
Things to Remember About Point of View in Your Writing

A **point of view** is the way someone sees, thinks, or feels about something.

Writing

- Use a fictional diary to give a detailed account of a character's point of view.
- Use a first-person narrator when you want to have everything in the story experienced from the narrator's point of view. Use *I*, *me*, and *my*.
- Use the third-person subjective point of view when you want to report the action mainly from one person's point of view without having that person narrate the story.
- Use the third-person omniscient point of view when you want to explain more than one person's thoughts, feelings, and motives.

Revising

Revise your writing by

- adding adverbs and adverbial phrases
- using connecting words, such as prepositions, conjunctions, and relative pronouns, to link sentences
- cutting out unnecessary, repetitious, misplaced, or dangling modifiers.
- replacing dull adjectives with fresh ones and similes
- using specific nouns and verbs

Writing diary entries

Details about everyday life tell a lot about a person's character. **Diaries** can give these details. A diary is usually a brief account of things that happen day by day. Trivial everyday happenings, thoughts, and dreams are all diary material. The best diaries are written freely and honestly, without any thought of how the writer might appear to other people. Many diaries of both famous and little-known people have been published. They are fascinating reading, because diaries are a unique way of revealing a person's point of view and the world he or she lives in.

A. To invent a fictional diary, you have to imagine a character's point of view. Imagine that you are a well-known actor or actress, musician, or politician on a world tour. Write a sample page of your diary. Give details about your work or your social life.

Date _____

_____

_____

_____

_____

_____

_____

Here's a wise saying:

　No one is a hero to his or her servant.

The saying means that it's pretty hard to make a hero or heroine out of someone you know well. Generally, you tend to admire people you don't know very well, like entertainers or sports figures. Once you get to know them, they often seem—too human.

B. What would your celebrity's secretary or tour guide feel like on this world tour? Write a diary page about the same day from the point of view of the secretary or guide. What is this person's private opinion of your celebrity?

_____

_____

_____

_____

_____

_____

_____

Notice that you've created two very different characters, both using the word *I*. Each *I* has a different **point of view.** They are **narrators** of scenes you've imagined. Many people think that the narrator is really the writer. But usually a narrator is as much a creation of the author's imagination as the story itself.

Also notice that you've written about the same day from two different points of view. Any event can be seen from several points of view.

C. Think once again about your celebrity. Can you imagine at least two other people who would have different points of view about the world tour? Jot them down below and add a few notes about each point of view.

_____

_____

_____

_____

_____

Good diaries always remain fresh. Each entry is usually written shortly after the events described took place. This is a portion of Samuel Pepys's diary written more than three hundred years ago. It remains as alive now as when it was first written.

> Anon the house grew full, and the candles light, and the King, Queen and all the ladies set. And it was indeed a glorious sight to see Mrs. Stewart in black and white lace and her head and shoulders dressed with diamonds. . . . Mrs. Stewart danced mighty finely, and many French dances, especially one the King called the New Dance, which was very pretty.

Diaries written ten, fifty, or a hundred years ago show history as it was lived. If you read a diary written during the Civil War, you realize that the war was not just an old story—for five years it was part of everyday life in America. Here's a quote from the diary of Sarah Morgan, who lived in Louisiana during the Civil War.

> Cousin Will saw one lying dead without a creature by to notice when he died. Another was dying, and muttering to himself as he lay too far gone to brush the flies out of his eyes and mouth, while no one was able to do it for him. Cousin Will helped him, though. . . . Oh, I wish these poor men were safe in their own land! It is heartbreaking to see them die here like dogs, with no one to say Godspeed.

Historical characters can become living people when you know what they felt and suffered.

D. Imagine someone living during the Civil War: for example, a general leading his men on an exhausting march, a Southern belle, an ex-slave fighting in the Union army, a plantation owner, or a foreign visitor. Write a diary entry that tells some of your character's experiences. What is your character's opinion of the war? Is your character involved or merely an observer? How does your character get along with the people around him or her?

E. You yourself are a historical figure. You are living history right now. Much of what you do and think could happen only today. You belong to the time you live in. Jot down events in a typical day. Then underline the events or phrases that show that you are living in the 1980s.

_____

_____

_____

_____

_____

_____

_____

_____

_____

Write On

Choose one of the activities below.

1. Think of a favorite historical character, someone you admire very much. Imagine that you were able to meet this person. Describe your historic meeting in a diary entry. What was this person like? What did you talk about? What were your feelings when you met this person? Was this person like what you expected?

2. A diary can show that a person's private life may be very different from her or his public life. A diary of a great singer, for example, could be filled with fears of not being good enough. Write a brief story in which you discover another person's diary. What do you learn about this person? How does it change your feelings about him or her?

Diaries are brief records of everyday life. A fictional diary can give a detailed account of a character's point of view.

Writing first-person and third-person narratives

Imagine that you are hearing a story read aloud. The voice you hear is the narrator's, telling the story in his or her own words. In a **first-person narrative,** the narrator uses the words *I, me, my,* and *mine.* In a third-person narrative, characters are referred to as *he* or *she.* In the **third-person narrative,** *I* is used only in dialogue or letters.

A. Read the following excerpts. Write *FP* if the passage comes from a first-person narrative and *TP* if it comes from a third-person narrative.

_____ 1. The schoolmaster was leaving the village, and everybody seemed sorry. (Thomas Hardy, *Jude the Obscure*)

_____ 2. I got another barber that comes over from Carterville and helps me out Saturdays, but the rest of the time I can get along all right alone. (Ring Lardner, "The Haircut")

_____ 3. When I was a child, I used to go to the seaside for the holidays. (Beatrix Potter, "Tale of Little Pig Robinson")

_____ 4. It is a truth universally acknowledged, that a single man in possession of a good fortune must be in want of a wife. (Jane Austen, *Pride and Prejudice*)

If you listen to the voices speaking in the lines above, you can tell that each narrator is very different. First-person narratives usually sound very much like a normal speaking voice. Third-person narratives are usually—though not always—more formal.

A writer is careful about choosing the right narrator for a story. The narrator gives the story a specific quality. Depending on the choice of words the narrator uses, the story can be serious or funny, simple or complicated. Sometimes it is a good idea to try several narrators for a story to find out which one suits it best.

Use the picture below to give you ideas for parts **B, C,** and **D.**

B. A remark about football turns a big Thanksgiving dinner into a family brawl. Write a paragraph, giving a humorous first-person account of the beginning of the dinner. The narrator is an involved participant in the football discussion in which some of the guests are supporting opposite teams, while some hate football.

_____

_____

_____

_____

_____

C. Now write another account of the dinner from the point of view of someone not involved in the fight: a small child or an out-of-town visitor. The fight is at its fiercest now: people are arguing about football, TV, and who took the last turkey wing.

_____

_____

_____

_____

_____

D. By dessert, no one is talking to anyone else. Describe the scene in a third-person account.

_____

_____

_____

_____

_____

A third-person narrative can be **subjective** or **omniscient.** In a subjective third-person narrative, the story is seen from the point of view of one person. In an omniscient third-person account, the narrator seems to know how all the characters feel.

E. Read the two quotes below. Write *O* if the passage seems to be written from an omniscient viewpoint and *S* if it seems to be a subjective narrative.

——— 1. Alice was beginning to get very tired of sitting by her sister on the bank, and of having nothing to do: once or twice she had peeped into the book her sister was reading, but it had no pictures or conversations in it, "and what is the use of a book," thought Alice, "without pictures or conversations?" (Lewis Carroll, *Alice's Adventures in Wonderland*)

——— 2. Once upon a time a father had two sons. The oldest was clever and wise and could do anything, but the younger son was stupid and couldn't understand anything—people used to look at him and say, "Oh, there's a son who is going to give his father trouble." (The Brothers Grimm, "The Boy Who Set Out to Learn Fear")

Have you ever been in an embarrassing situation—for example, walking down the street with a gaping hole in your jeans, or forgetting lines in a school play? Your "point of view" in those situations becomes wildly off-target because you're nervous. You may think that everybody is staring at you or talking about you.

A character's point of view can provide a story in itself. A story which concentrates on a character's feelings and thoughts is often called a **character study.**

F. Write a third-person subjective account of a character who has to deliver ten thousand dollars to a large train station. The money is stored in a large supermarket bag so it won't look suspicious. Still, the character thinks that every passerby knows there's money in that bag. Describe your character's fears and suspicions.

————————————————————————————————

————————————————————————————————

————————————————————————————————

————————————————————————————————

————————————————————————————————

————————————————————————————————

————————————————————————————————

————————————————————————————————

G. Any group of strangers gathered together—in a waiting room, for example, or on a bus or ship—can be the subject of a story. Although they are physically close, their thoughts and lives are separate. Write a paragraph or two from an omniscient viewpoint: describe two strangers, and give some details about their thoughts. Do they notice one another? Are they preoccupied with worries? Daydreaming?

_____

_____

_____

_____

_____

_____

_____

_____

_____

_____

Choose one of the story ideas you used in this lesson: the Thanksgiving fight, the money in the bag, or the two strangers in one place. Work out a plot with a climax and a conclusion. Then decide from which point of view you will narrate the story. On another sheet of paper, write your story. Keep your point of view consistent.

A narrative may be written from the first-person, third-person subjective, or third-person omniscient point of view, depending on the writer's goals.

Writing about your life

The story of your life is the story you know best of all. Unlike most writing assignments, this one requires no investigation of secondary sources. As the writer of your **autobiography,** you may find that you have far too much information to handle well. Where should you begin? What are the important events? Who were the important influences? How can you begin to put it all on paper?

You could of course, simply begin with your earliest memories and write everything that you can recall in the sequence that the events actually happened. But an autobiography is more than simply the retelling of events in your life.

Your task in this lesson will be to select an important phase from your past, describe it in detail, and answer the question: What did it mean?

What is a phase? In this case, a **phase** is simply a portion of your life with a beginning and an end. A summer might be a phase in your life. Your adaptation to a school or the birth of one of your brothers or sisters could also be a phase.

A. Jot down a few events or feelings in your life that you particularly remember.

_____

_____

_____

_____

B. Choose one of the events from part **A** to become the phase you will write about. In the space below, briefly describe the phase. Note the events and the approximate dates on which the phase started and ended.

_____

_____

_____

_____

_____

C. What was the nature of this phase? Did you learn something about yourself? Did you grow up, or learn a new skill?

_____

_____

_____

_____

_____

D. Now that you have begun to define the change you experienced during this phase of your life, you should write a statement of the theme of this autobiographical phase. The theme could be friendship, learning, or loss. It should capture the meaning of the phase for you.

_____

_____

_____

In order for your readers to know how you changed during this phase, they should have some idea of what you were like before the phase.

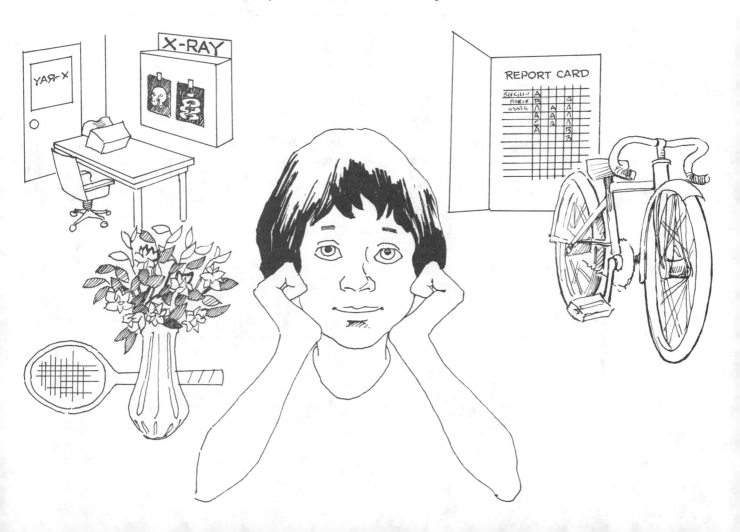

E. Describe briefly your feelings before this phase. In your description make it clear why this phase was important to you.

_____

_____

_____

_____

F. The changes you underwent during this phase were largely produced by important people and events at that time in your life. List the persons that influenced you during this period. Describe each person and the particular events that person is linked to. Then describe the influence that person had on you.

Person: _____

_____

_____

Person: _____

_____

_____

Person: _____

_____

_____

G. List in chronological order the important events that took place during this phase of your life. After each event, describe your reaction to it.

Event: _____

_____

Event: _____

_____

Event: _____

_____

Event: _____

Event: _____

H. You learned how it is possible to describe the same event from different points of view. Other people may have different viewpoints about your phase than you do. In fact, your own point of view may have changed. You may have been unhappy about this period of your life while you were living it and discovered later how valuable it was to you. Your autobiography should be written from your present point of view. What is your viewpoint about this phase of your life now?

_____

_____

_____

_____

_____

I. What makes you remember this phase today? Do people remind you? Are you reminded by sights and sounds that recall that period of your life? Do you compare present experiences to that time in your life?

_____

_____

_____

_____

_____

Write On

Using the ideas and information you have written above, you should be able to write several paragraphs about your autobiographical phase. As you write, try to combine the telling of the events with your interpretation of their significance.

An autobiography is the story of one's life: it tells both the events and the significance of those events in a person's life.

Revising

Polishing your writing

When you have finished your first draft of a story or an essay, it is a good idea to reread what you have written and revise it until it's as good as you can make it.

A. The rules below review some of the guidelines for revising that you have studied in this book. Use them to help you revise the sentences beneath each rule.

1. Add adverbs and adverbial phrases to sentences to give specific information about how, when, and where.

   The batter hit the ball.

   _____

   _____

2. Use connecting words, such as prepositions, conjunctions, and relative pronouns, to link sentences and make relationships clear.

   Shop for winter clothes now. Spring clothes are already out.
   Winter clothes are on clearance sale. You can get some real bargains.

   _____

   _____

   _____

3. Don't overload your sentences with too many modifiers.

   On top of the old, antique, battered desk lay an old worn diary which was an old brown book with two faded photographs about fifty years old inside of the diary.

   _____

   _____

4. Rewrite sentences to correct misplaced or dangling modifiers.

   Desperately clinging to life rafts, the Coast Guard cutter approached the survivors.
   Wrapped in blankets to keep warm, the cutter headed into port.

   _____

   _____

   _____

5. Replace dull adjectives with fresh adjectives and similes.

   Staying in the big old house made Kerry feel strange.

   _____

   _____

6. Use specific nouns and verbs to make your sentences clear and accurate.

   Everyone will go there tonight.

   _____

   _____

7. Combine sentences and omit or change repeated words to improve paragraph rhythm.

   I eat breakfast. I get on my bicycle. I ride north. I ride on country roads. The roads are long and winding. I see woods. I see farms. The farms have red barns. The barns are off in the distance.

   _____

   _____

   _____

   _____

B. Revise the paragraph below, combining sentences and changing words until it sounds just right to you.

   The night was dark. The night was chilly. She heard something at her window. Suddenly, a figure leapt there. Screaming loudly, the bedroom door flew open. It was the police. They were there. She was safe.

   _____

   _____

   _____

   _____

   _____

Write On
Go over all the papers you wrote this year and pick one you would like to improve. Revise it, keeping in mind the guidelines you have studied in this book. When your paper says just what you want it to say, make a neat copy.

Revise your writing until it says exactly what you want it to say.

1. Read the paragraph below. Then write a first-person narrative about the incident from the point of view of one of the people involved.

   A commercial jet carrying 348 people made an emergency landing yesterday when the landing gear did not work properly. Airport officials say the pilot made a skillful "bellylanding." Some minor injuries were reported, but no one was seriously hurt. Passengers were quickly evacuated from the plane.

2. Read this diary excerpt. Tell whose point of view the excerpt could describe.

   Today, the egg shows signs of hatching. If the egg doesn't hatch within 72 hours, I'll have to help it, but I don't want to rush things. I'm not going to leave the lab until it's over. If the chick hatches, it will be the first crested sandhopper ever born in captivity.

   _____

3. Read each quote below. Write S if it is a subjective narrative, or O if it is omniscient.

   _____ a. When Leslie entered the office, she saw a brusque, stocky man who barely gave her a glance. She gulped and wondered what chance she had to win the music scholarship.

   _____ b. Derek and Fran soon launched into their favorite topic: Dr. Dower. Unfortunately, both of them were too busy to notice Mrs. Dower, who had sat down in the row ahead of them.

4. Revise this paragraph.

   My parents were both in the Army. They traveled a lot. I was born in France. My brother was born in Germany. Living in different places, other cultures became familiar to us. Making new friends was sometimes hard and difficult. It was an absorbing, interesting life.

   _____

   _____

   _____

   _____

   _____

Writing Handbook

When your writing says exactly what you want it to say, it is a good idea to proofread to look for errors you might have made in capitalization, punctuation, or word usage. The following pages include rules for using capital letters, punctuation marks, and word forms correctly. Use this handbook as a reference whenever you have any questions. When you feel you know the rules, turn to page 124 and take the proofreading test there.

PART 1 CAPITALIZATION

1. The first word of every sentence begins with a capital letter.

    The players were in a huddle. What would they do?

    The first word of a direct quotation begins with a capital letter.

    The quarterback said, "Let's fake a pass."

2. In the titles or subtitles of works, the first, the last, and any important words begin with capital letters. "Important words" means all words except *a, an, the*; coordinate conjunctions; prepositions of four letters or less; and *to* in an infinitive.

    I Know Why the Caged Bird Sings (book)
    The Merchant of Venice (play)
    "I Like to See It Lap the Miles" (poem)
    the *Daily Clarion* (newspaper; *the* not part of title)

3. Every word or abbreviation in a proper noun begins with a capital letter (except *of, the, and*). A proper noun names a particular person, animal, place, or thing.

    James E. Carter, Jr.
    Bogotá, Colombia (city/country)
    Pacific Ocean (body of water)
    Merritt Parkway (road)
    the *Monitor* (boat)
    the Magna Charta (document)
    Sunkist oranges (brand name)
    Friday, May 11 (day/month)

    Passover (holiday)
    the American Revolution (historic event)
    Christianity (religion)
    the Red Cross (organization)
    Jefferson High School (institution)
    the Democratic Party (political party)
    the Photography Club (club)
    Sears, Roebuck and Co. (company)

    Do not begin a common noun with a capital letter, even when it refers to a proper noun just mentioned. A common noun is a general noun (see page 120).

    We swam in the Pacific Ocean.   The ocean was rough.

4. Titles and ranks (and their abbreviations) begin with capital letters when they occur with names.

    General Douglas MacArthur
    Professor Emilia Ruiz

    Dr. Horace Chang, Jr.
    Mary, Queen of Scots

Ranks or titles that appear alone do not begin with capital letters.

The <u>q</u>ueen gave a speech.　　　Where's the <u>d</u>octor?

You may capitalize family relationship words that appear alone if they are used as names.

I asked <u>D</u>ad for a loan.

5. Do not capitalize the words for directions unless they are being used as parts of names or to name specific geographic places.

They went <u>w</u>est.　　They live on <u>W</u>est Street.　　They visited the <u>W</u>est.

PART 2 PUNCTUATION

Apostrophes (')

1. An apostrophe is used to show the possessive form of a noun.

Reiko<u>'</u>s ring　　the horses<u>'</u> saddles　　the men<u>'</u>s lockers

2. An apostrophe is used in a contraction to show that a letter or letters have been left out.

don<u>'</u>t (do not)　　let<u>'</u>s (let us)　　they<u>'</u>re (they are)

Colons (:)

1. A colon is used to introduce a list.

The campers took the following items<u>:</u> one tent, three sleeping bags, a stove, and some pots.

2. A colon is sometimes used to introduce a direct quotation. (A comma would also be correct; a colon simply makes a stronger pause.)

Abraham Lincoln said<u>:</u> "The ballot is stronger than the bullet."

Commas (,)

1. A comma is used to separate two independent clauses linked by a coordinate conjunction.

The car stopped<u>,</u> and a woman jumped out.

2. Commas are used to separate items in a series.

She carried flowers<u>,</u> chocolates<u>,</u> and fruit.

It is not necessary to use commas in a series if coordinate conjunctions are used between all items.

Bring flowers or chocolates or fruit.

3. A comma is used to separate coordinate adjectives (adjectives of equal force that separately modify the same noun).

An old<u>,</u> tattered book lay on the desk.

Do not use a comma to separate adjectives that are not coordinate.

Its cover was dull olive green.

4. Commas are used to set off modifying phrases and clauses when they come before the main clause.

> To solve the case, Miss Marple needed more clues.
> Standing outside the door, she heard every word.
> Behind the bookcase next to the far wall, there was a safe.
> When she entered the room, the safe was open.

A comma is not required after a short introductory adverbial phrase.

> Behind the bookcase there was a safe.

5. Commas are used to set off nonrestrictive modifying appositives, phrases, and clauses. A nonrestrictive element is one that merely adds information to the word it follows.

> My favorite singer, Diana Ross, made that record.
> One skater, wearing a red scarf, is waving to you.
> That car, which has a dented fender, should be repaired.

Do not set off restrictive modifying appositives, phrases, and clauses with commas. A restrictive element restricts, or limits, the meaning of the word it follows.

> We saw the singer Diana Ross in person.
> The skater wearing a red scarf is my cousin.
> The car that has a dented fender belongs to Tim.

6. Commas are used to set off parenthetic words and expressions—words and expressions that interrupt the sentence.

> No, I am not going. I will, of course, if you insist.

7. Commas are used to set off a direct quotation that is not a grammatical part of the entire sentence.

> The coach said, "Winning isn't everything."

When the quotation is a grammatical part of the sentence, do not use commas unless the sentence structure makes them necessary.

> The coach told the team that "winning isn't everything."

8. Commas are used in dates to separate the day's name from the month, the day's number from the year, and the end of the date from the rest of the sentence.

> On June 19, 1846, the first organized baseball game was played.

9. Commas are used in street addresses to separate the street from the town or city, the town or city from the state or country, the state from the country, and the end of the address from the rest of the sentence.

> We moved to 129 Union Street, Columbus, Ohio, two years ago.
> My sister went to Cambridge, England, for her junior year in college.

10. Commas are used to set off a person's title or rank when it follows the name.

> Martin Luther King, Jr., was a great man.

11. Commas are used to set off the name of a person directly addressed (spoken to).

> Fetch the ball, Rags.   Brigitta, please answer the phone.

Exclamation Points (!)

An exclamation point always follows an exclamation and sometimes follows an imperative sentence.

> How lovely you look!   Nuts!   Stop that!

Italics/Underlining

1. The titles of longer works—books, longer poems, plays, films, works of art, symphonies, magazines, and newspapers—are italicized (or underlined in handwriting or typewriting). The names of ships, planes, and spacecraft are also italicized (or underlined).

> *Frankenstein* was written by Mary Shelley in 1818.
> The space module *Eagle* was the first craft to land on the moon.

2. Words as words and letters as letters are italicized (or underlined).

> What word besides *abstemious* has *a*, *e*, *i*, *o*, and *u* in order?

Periods (.)

1. A period always follows a declarative sentence and usually follows an imperative sentence.

> Five English words begin with *gh*. Name them.

2. Periods are used in most abbreviations. (Note: *Miss* is not an abbreviation.)

> Mrs. Mr.   Rev. Sgt. Ph.D. N.J. Mich.
> Rd.   Tpke. Can. Eur. A.D.   P.M. R.S.V.P.

Some abbreviations and acronyms (words formed from the first letters of each important word in a term) do not use periods. Official post office abbreviations accompanied by zip codes do not use periods. If in doubt, check your dictionary.

> rpm (revolutions per minute)   Norfolk, VA 23518
> NBC (National Broadcasting Company)   Springfield, MO 65803

Question Marks (?)

A question mark follows an interrogative sentence.

> What is the tallest mountain in the world?

Quotation Marks (" ") (' ')

1. Quotation marks are used to set off a direct quotation.

> Luis asked, "Did you see my keys?"

2. Quotation marks are used to set off the titles of stories, short poems, articles, chapters, essays, songs, TV shows, and other short works.

> "The Lottery" is a story by Shirley Jackson.

3. Quotation marks are used to set off coined words or words intended to mean something different from what they normally mean.

The "orchestra" consisted of two guitars and a kazoo.

4. Single quotation marks are used inside double quotation marks.

"I hope to appear on 'The Gong Show' soon," said Uncle Egbert.

NOTE: A comma or a period *always* goes inside of a closing quotation mark. A semicolon or a colon *always* goes outside a closing quotation mark. A question mark or an exclamation point goes either inside or outside a closing quotation mark, depending on whether or not it is part of the quotation.

He sang "Three Blind Mice." We begged, "Will you please stop?"
Kristin said, "I can't stand it"; I said, "I agree."
Does he know "Row, Row Your Boat"?

Semicolons (;)

1. A semicolon is used to separate two independent, related clauses when a coordinate conjunction is not used.

The car stopped; immediately a woman jumped out.

2. Semicolons are used to separate items in a series when at least one element already has a comma.

We have cheese, tuna, or egg sandwiches; tossed salad; and sherbet.

PART 3   USAGE

Adjectives and Adverbs

1. An adjective modifies a noun, a pronoun, or a gerund.

His loud snoring woke the whole family.

An adverb or adverbial phrase tells how, how often, when, or where. Most adverbs and adverbials modify verbs.

Trucks rumble noisily past my house every morning.

A common error that many people make is to use adjectives when they should use adverbs. Remember, adjectives do not modify verbs.

Trucks rumble noisily (not *noisy*).   She dances well (not *good*).

2. Both adjectives and adverbs can be used to show comparisons. There are two degrees of comparison: comparative and superlative. Comparative degree is used to compare two items. Superlative degree is used to compare three or more items. Rules for showing comparison are as follows.

a. For all one-syllable and some two-syllable adjectives and adverbs, add -er for the comparative and -est for the superlative.

Peter came early.
Vera came earlier than Pete.
Ichi came earliest of all.

The lamp is bright.
The streetlight is brighter than the lamp.
The moon is brightest of all.

b. For all other adjectives and adverbs, use the word *more* for the comparative and the word *most* for the superlative.

Pete walks quickly.
Vera walks <u>more</u> quickly than Pete.
Ichi walks <u>most</u> quickly of all.

The flowered dress is vivid.
The yellow dress is <u>more</u> vivid.
The red dress is <u>most</u> vivid of all.

c. A few adjectives and adverbs show comparative and superlative degrees by changing form completely.

	Comparative	Superlative
good } well	better	best
bad	worse	worst
little (meaning *few*)	less	least

A common error that many people make is to use a double comparative or superlative form.

Vera walks <u>more faster</u> than Pete.   The sun is the <u>most brightest</u> star.

Agreement

1. A present-tense verb must agree with its subject. The simple form of the verb is used with *I*, *you*, and all plural subjects. The *s* form is used with all singular subjects except *I* and *you*.

I <u>like</u> peanuts.
You <u>like</u> peanuts.
Squirrels <u>like</u> peanuts.

He like<u>s</u> peanuts.
Elinor like<u>s</u> peanuts
That bluejay like<u>s</u> peanuts.

Sometimes the word *Here* or *There* is used as a sentence starter. In this case, the verb agrees with the subject that follows.

Here <u>is</u> the bacon, and there <u>are</u> the eggs.

For more information on present-tense verb forms, see page 122.

2. A pronoun must agree with the noun or other pronoun to which it refers.

When Aunt Lula came, <u>she</u> brought gifts.   (*She* refers to *Aunt Lula*).
I opened my gift. <u>It</u> was a tape recorder.   (*It* refers to *gift*).
The twins loved <u>their</u> new sweaters.   (*Their* refers to *twins*).

For more information on pronouns, see page 121.

3. Many people make agreement errors with singular indefinite pronouns (see the list on page 121). Remember: A singular indefinite pronoun is not affected by any adjective phrase that comes after it.

<u>Neither</u> of the boys like<u>s</u> <u>his</u> old sweaters anymore. (Do not be confused by the adjective phrase *of the boys*; the subject *neither* is singular.)
<u>Everybody</u> <u>was</u> surprised to hear <u>his or her</u> voice on tape.

A few indefinite pronouns may be either singular or plural (see the list on page 121). With these pronouns, the adjective phrases are helpful.

<u>All</u> of the <u>food</u> <u>is</u> gone.   <u>All</u> of the <u>peanuts</u> <u>are</u> gone.

4. Nouns or pronouns joined by *and* form a compound expression that is plural.

<u>Aunt Lula and Uncle Ben</u> <u>like</u> to cook.
<u>They and I</u> <u>make</u> a good chili.

If the expression joined by *and* names a single thing, it is singular.

<u>Peanut butter and jelly</u> <u>is</u> my favorite sandwich.

5. Singular nouns or pronouns joined by *or* or *nor* form a compound expression that is singular.

Neither <u>Ray nor Roy</u> <u>likes</u> <u>his</u> peanut butter sandwich.

Plural nouns or pronouns joined by *or* or *nor* form a compound expression that is plural.

Neither <u>the twins nor their friends</u> <u>like</u> <u>their</u> peanut butter sandwiches.

You should avoid constructions in which a singular is joined to a plural by *or* or *nor*. However, the rule for such a case is that the verb or any pronoun agrees with the closer word.

Acceptable: Neither the twins nor <u>Aunt Lula</u> <u>likes</u> <u>her</u> peanut butter sandwich.
Better: The twins don't like their peanut butter sandwich, and neither does Aunt Lula.
Acceptable: Neither Aunt Lula nor the <u>twins</u> <u>like</u> <u>their</u> peanut butter sandwiches.
Better: Aunt Lula doesn't like her peanut butter sandwich, and neither do the twins.

Comparison (See Adjectives and Adverbs on page 117.)

Dangling Modifiers (See Unit 3, page 47.)

Double Negatives

1. Using more than one negative word in a clause is considered a mistake.

They don't want nothing.   should be changed to:
They don't want anything. OR They want nothing.

2. The words *barely, hardly,* and *scarcely* are half negatives and also should not appear together with another negative word.

They hardly ate nothing.   should be changed to:
They hardly ate anything.

Fragments

A sentence fragment is a group of words that, though punctuated like a sentence, does not express a complete thought.

A large bouquet of roses.   As soon as I got home.

In general, you should avoid sentence fragments in your writing.
However, fragments are sometimes acceptable—in realistic dialogue, for example.

"What did you buy your mother?"   "A large bouquet of roses."
"When did you give them to her?"   "As soon as I got home."

Misplaced Modifiers (See Unit 3, page 47.)

Negatives (See Double Negatives, page 119.)

Nouns

1. A noun names a person, an animal, a place, a thing, or an idea.

    The <u>boy</u> and his <u>dog</u> enjoyed their new <u>freedom</u> in the <u>country</u>.

2. A noun can be either common or proper. A proper noun is the name of a particular person, animal, place, or thing. The first letter is always capitalized (see page 113).

    Brigitta   Rags   Bogotá   Chevrolet

    A common noun is any other noun.

    girl   dog   city   car

3. A noun can be singular (one) or plural (more than one). The rules for spelling the plural forms of nouns follow.

    a. In most cases, the plural form is made by adding -*s* to the singular.

       girl, girl<u>s</u>   dog, dog<u>s</u>   car, car<u>s</u>

    b. When a singular noun ends in a consonant plus *y*, the plural is formed by changing the *y* to *i* and adding -*es*.

       city, cit<u>ies</u>   factory, factor<u>ies</u>   country, countr<u>ies</u>

    c. When a singular noun ends in a consonant plus *o*, the plural is sometimes formed by adding -*es*. Check your dictionary.

       torpedo, torped<u>oes</u>   echo, ech<u>oes</u>   motto, mott<u>oes</u>

    d. When a singular noun ends in *f* or *fe*, the plural is sometimes formed by changing the *f* or *fe* to *v* and adding -*es*. Check your dictionary.

       life, li<u>ves</u>   shelf, shel<u>ves</u>   wife, wi<u>ves</u>

    e. Irregular plurals are formed in various ways. Whenever you are not sure, check your dictionary.

       tooth, <u>teeth</u>   phenomenon, <u>phenomena</u>   sheep, <u>sheep</u>

4. A noun can be made into a possessive to show ownership. A singular noun is made into a possessive by adding an apostrophe (') and an *s*.

    the thief<u>'s</u> mask   the boss<u>'s</u> office   Bess<u>'s</u> scarf

    To form the possessive of a plural noun that ends in *s*, just add an apostrophe.

    the thieves<u>'</u> masks   the bosses<u>'</u> offices   the girls<u>'</u> scarves

If the plural form does not end in s, add an apostrophe and an s to form the possessive.

the sheep's wool   the people's choice   the children's games

Plurals (See Agreement, page 118, and Nouns, page 120.)

Possession (See Nouns, page 120, and Pronouns below.)

Pronouns

1. Pronouns have subject, object, and possessive forms. Many people have difficulty using the forms of pronouns correctly, especially when they occur in compound subjects or objects.

   a. Use subjective forms of pronouns that are subjects of sentences or predicate nominatives (following linking verbs).

   Dad and <u>I</u> mowed the lawn.   The car washers were Milt and <u>she</u>.

   b. Use objective forms of pronouns that are objects of verbs, prepositions, or verbals.

   Let's take Lorraine and <u>them</u> to the game.   (direct object)
   Send Brenda or <u>him</u> the package.   (indirect object)
   Throw the pass to Lacey or <u>me</u>.   (object of a preposition)
   After seeing Jamie and <u>her</u>, Ralph left.   (object of a verbal)

2. Possessive pronouns, like possessive nouns, show ownership. But unlike possessive nouns, possessive pronouns do not have any apostrophes.

   <u>His</u> tickets are now <u>theirs</u>.   <u>My</u> watch lost <u>its</u> crystal.

   A common error people make is to confuse certain possessive pronouns with contractions that they sound like.

   <u>Their</u> house is oddly furnished.   (*Their* is a possessive pronoun.)
   <u>They're</u> buying a new three-legged chair.   (*They're* is a contraction for *they are*.)
   <u>Your</u> watch is slow.   (*Your* is a possessive pronoun.)
   <u>You're</u> always late.   (*You're* is a contraction for *you are*.)

3. An indefinite pronoun refers to an unspecified person, place, or thing. Most indefinite pronouns are always singular, some can be singular or plural, and a few are always plural. For a discussion of agreement with indefinite pronouns, see page 118.

INDEFINITE PRONOUNS					
Always Singular			**Singular or Plural**		**Always Plural**
another	everybody	no one	all	most	both
anybody	everyone	nothing	any	none	few
anyone	everything	one	enough	some	many
anything	much	other	more	such	several
each	neither	somebody			
either	nobody	someone			
		something			

Run Ons

A run-on sentence is a sentence in which two or more independent clauses are joined together without correct punctuation.

> Pablo's pencil broke he used his pen.
> Pablo's pencil broke, he used his pen.

The above run-on sentence could be corrected as follows:

a. Add a semicolon to show that the two independent clauses are related. (You may also add a conjunctive adverb.)

> Pablo's pencil broke; he used his pen.
> Pablo's pencil broke; therefore, he used his pen.

b. Add a coordinate conjunction between the two independent clauses.

> Pablo's pencil broke, and he used his pen.

c. Add a subordinate conjunction to one of the clauses.

> When Pablo's pencil broke, he used his pen.

d. If the two independent clauses are unrelated, make them into separate sentences.

> Run on: Pablo's pencil broke I used green ink.
> Corrected: Pablo's pencil broke. I used green ink.

Verbs

Verbs have five forms.

a. The simple form is used for present tense with plural subjects, *I*, and *you*. (It is sometimes called the plural form.) It is also used after all helping verbs except forms of *have* and *be*.

> I sneeze.   They sneeze.   Will you sneeze?

b. The *-s* form is the simple form plus *-s*. It is used for present tense with singular subjects (except *I* and *you*). (It is sometimes called the singular form.)

> Molly sneezes.   She sneezes.

c. The *-ing* form, or the present participle, is the simple form plus *-ing*. It is used after the helping verb *be* to form the progressive tenses. For spelling changes in the *ing* form, consult your dictionary.

d. The *-ed* ending is used for both the past tense and the past participle, but these are actually different forms. The past tense *-ed* form stands alone.

> He sneezed.   They sneezed.   We sneezed.   I sneezed.

Notice that the same past-tense form is used for all subjects. The only exception is *be*.

I was   You (or plural subjects) were   He (or singular subjects) was

For spelling changes in the past tense, consult your dictionary.

e. The past participle (also -*ed* ending) is used after the helping verb *have*.

> I <u>have sneezed</u>.   She <u>has sneezed</u>.   I <u>had sneezed</u>.

f. Irregular verbs are verbs that do not form their past tense and past participle (-*ed*) forms in the regular way. The term does not apply to mere spelling changes (*carry* to *carried*, for example) but to complete irregularity. Often, irregular verbs have two different forms for past tense and past participle.

> I <u>went</u> there; I <u>have gone</u> there.

For irregular verb forms, consult your dictionary.

NOTE: Make sure you do not confuse the simple past tense with the past participle when they are different.

> Wrong: I have wrote the letter.
> Correct: I have written the letter.

PART IV Letter Forms

1. Most business letters have six parts arranged in the following way.

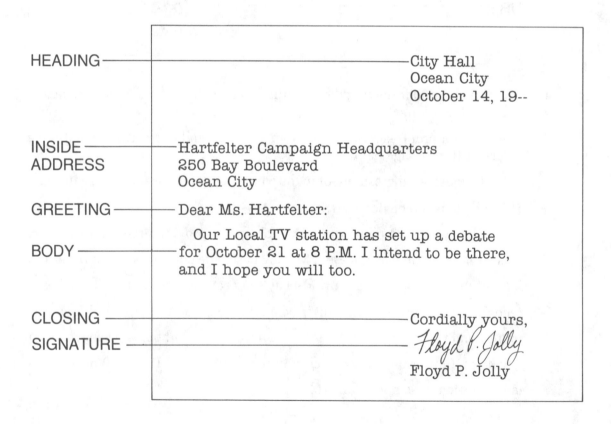

2. A colon is used following the greeting of a formal business letter.

3. Most friendly letters have five parts arranged in the following way.

HEADING ——————————————— Villa Wechsler
Nice, France
May 1, 19—

GREETING ——————— Dear Mother,

BODY ——————— Unfortunately, the weather here has been quite sunny. But I did a lot of good work during the March rains. I'd love to have you see my latest paintings. Perhaps you can come for a visit this summer. I can promise you lots of water sports.

CLOSING ——————————————— With love,
SIGNATURE ——————————————— *Wanda*
Wanda

4. Commas are used following the greeting of a friendly letter, and following the closing of any letter.

A. How good a proofreader are you? Can you find and correct the twenty-five errors in the passage below?

The most popularest rodent in the world mickey mouse, was born in 1928. He maked his screen debut in Steamboat Willie, the first cartoon to use sound Walt Disney, the man who drawed Mickey also provided the mouses voice. Since his first film was released. Mickey has made countless, other films and has became world famous. Now Mickey's big ears bow tie and white gloves is recognized everywhere. Can their be anyone who don't know and love this mouse among mouses. the ageless star now have two homes. Disneyland in Anaheim, California, was opened on July 17 1955, and Disney World in Orlando florida, was opened in 1971.

Unit 1

Lesson 1 (pages 2–5)

A. 5, 7, 1, 3, 10, 8, 9, 4, 2, 6

B. 1. the controversial underwater painter
2. In the paragraph you should have underlined sentences 2 and 3. The underlined sentences help to show a connection between the events by telling us what effect water had in shaping her career.

C. Whenever you see this symbol, check with your teacher.

D.

E. L or C   C
   C   L
   C   L
   L   C
   C   L

F.

Lesson 2 (pages 6–9)

A. 1. The movie scene might begin with Captain Corcoran floating around in his space capsule.
2. his first pole vault.
3. The flashback reveals his longstanding desire to escape from gravity.

B.

C. 1. She might discover the approach of the Earth Raiders.
2. The author can create a fast pace and a tension between the two events.

D.

E. 1. what caused the whirring sound and what the "gum" really is
2.

F.

Lesson 3 (pages 10–13)

A. I. The earliest comics
     A. "Hogan's Alley" first comic in 1895
     B. "Mutt and Jeff" first daily in 1907
  II. Adventure strips of the thirties
     A. "Dick Tracy" started in 1931
     B. "Superman" and "Prince Valiant" follow in thirties
 III. Modern comics
     A. Some old comics continue in the 70's
     B. New comics combine humor with satire

B. I. Folk music   III. Rock music
  II. Show music   IV. Country/Western music

C. I. Folk music
     A. Famous folk singers
       1. Woody Guthrie

       2. Joan Baez
       3. Pete Seeger
     B. Imported folk songs
       1. Mexican songs
       2. English ballads
       3. West Indian calypso
     C. Songs native to America
       1. Western prairie songs
       2. New England sea chanteys
       3. Black American spirituals

D. 1. The main idea of the paragraph is that American folk songs developed out of work situations.
2. The subhead that was left out was: New England sea chanteys
3. You should have underlined the last two sentences.
4. These sentences belong under I. A. 1.

E.   **F.**

Lesson 4 (pages 14–15)

A.

B. You might have crossed out the following adverbs: *easily, lightly, strongly, closely, softly, gradually, attentively, regularly, bravely, directly.* Substitutions will vary.

C.

Unit 2

Lesson 1 (pages 18–21)

A. 3   **B.** 2   **C.** 5, 2, 7, 1, 4, 6, 3

D. 1. effect   2. first

E. Your answer for the first paragraph should be similar to one of these: *The magician's first night on stage was a disaster. (effect)* OR *That magician needed more practice. (cause)* Your answer to the second paragraph should be similar to this: *The farmer lost the entire crop of peas that year. (effect)*

F.

Lesson 2 (pages 22–25)

A. 6, 3, 1, 8, 4, 2, 7, 5
The thief was the chauffeur.

B.   **C.**

D. You might have listed haunted houses, mountaintops, wolves, sharks, hurricanes, fires, and so on.

E. **F.** **G.**

Lesson 3 (pages 26–29)

A. Your answer should have been that Carlotta Braun's conclusion is not warranted because there are too many variables: the mice were not the same size and they were each given different food.

B. 1. Your answer might be that sunflower seeds grow best when they are exposed to lots of sunlight.
2. Your answer should be that foot blisters are caused by friction, not by the color of the socks or shoes worn.

125

C. 1. F   3. C   5. C   7. F
    2. C   4. F   6. C   8. F

D.

Lesson 4 (pages 30–31)

A.

Unit 3

Lesson 1 (pages 34–37)

A. 1. Bowling: The person who knocks down the most pins with a ball in ten frames, or rounds, is the winner.
2. Basketball: The team that throws the most balls into the basket wins.
3. Dominoes: Players must try to get rid of their dominos by playing those with sections identical to the end dominoes on the board.
4. Football: Teams score points by getting the ball over the opposing team's goal line and by kicking the ball over the opposing team's goal post.

B. You should have put an X next to 1 and 4.

C.   **D.**   **E.**   **F.**   **G.**

Lesson 2 (pages 38–41)

A. 1. Both paragraphs are about the effect the hot sun has on the people who live in the city.
2. The mood of the first paragraph is anger and hostility.
3. tempers, arguments, sticky clothes
4. The mood of the second paragraph is one of serenity or joy.
5. people in parks, cheery words, picnicking

B.   **C.**   **D.**   **E.**

Lesson 3 (pages 42–45)

A.   **B.**   **C.**   **D.**   **E.**

Lesson 4 (pages 46–47)

A. Your answers should be similar to these:
1. A dog-eared old book with a stained cover lay on the dusty desk.
2. A crowd of gaily dressed couples danced as the music blared and lights flashed.
3. The half-frozen children huddled under the warm quilt because the room was unheated.

B. 1. As I came in view of the landing sight, my fears were confirmed.
2. Armed aliens, who were ready to attack at any moment, crouched behind the hills.
3. My partner Lom, who was not feeling well, decided to stay in the spaceship.
4. Since the radio was in Lom's pocket, I could not use it to get help.
5. I knew that someday in the comfort of my own home I would tell of my adventures in space.

Unit 4

Lesson 1 (pages 50–53)

A. 1. A dhow is a type of sailing vessel used by Arabs.

126

2. A blintze is like a thin pancake folded around a filling such as cheese or fruit.
3. A serape is a blanketlike shawl.
4. A samisen is a guitarlike Japanese musical instrument.

B.   **C.**   **D.**   **E.**

F. 1. They both have rows of desks, ringing phones, scurrying reporters.
2. A modern office has humming electric typewriters, and typewriters which are tied into computer screens.

Lesson 2 (pages 54–57)

A. 1. like a thunderbolt he falls
2. The eagle's sudden flight is compared to a sudden bolt of lightning.
3. "He clasps the crag with crooked hands" or "The wrinkled sea beneath him crawls."

B.

C. 1. M - Just as food nourishes the body, knowledge nourishes the mind, or soul.
2. S - Youth is like a summer morn because summer is the time when nature blooms. Age is like winter because nature begins to wither and die just like an old person.
3. P - Money is given human qualities of serving man, but when it is allowed to control man it is a bad master.
4. P - The rain is being compared to someone singing a lullaby because when rain falls steadily against a windowpane it can have a soothing rhythm.

D.

E. Your answers may be similar to these:
1. Like a fearless eagle, he confidently went about feathering his nest.
2. She was an eager beaver, always ready to build a new dam.
3. The clock's ticking reminded him of the beating of a drum.
4. Her smile was the sunshine that brightened our days.

F.

Lesson 3 (pages 58–61)

A. 1. hen   6. money
2. bird   7. photographer
3. old   8. restaurant
4. simple   9. mountain
5. sun   10. dance

B. Here are some possible examples. Your answers may be different.
1. boy : girl   5. carpenter : furniture
2. baby : mother   6. tomato : salad
3. crooked : straight   7. cook : kitchen =
4. singer : chorus   judge : courtroom

C.

D. 1. Your answer may be similar to this:
Lack of decision may cost you your life.
2.

E. Your answer may be similar to this:
Action speaks louder than words.

F.

Lesson 4 (pages 62–63)

A. Here are some possible answers:
1. The winding freight train chugged slowly out of the dismal freightyard and began a lengthy journey to the East Coast.
2. The luxurious golf course was overrun by enthusiastic fans who wanted to observe every move made by their favorite professional golfers.
3. The timid girl stared at her new pink dancing shoes as a brawny young man in a black tuxedo strode toward her.

B. 1. brooding ⇨   5. scratchy ⇨
2. grouchy ⇨   6. cracking or cracked ⇨
3. carpeted ⇨   7. ⇨
4. howling ⇨   8. ⇨

C. ⇨

Unit 5

Lesson 1 (pages 66–69)

A. 1. when, who, what
2. who, what
3. who, what, when
4. what, who, when

B. ⇨

C. 1. F - This statement could be checked by checking data on San Francisco's and Bolivia's sales tax.
2. O - This statement is an opinion because it uses such words as *small fortune, dirty,* and *nasty.*
3. O - This statement is an opinion because it uses such phrases as "a waste of time."
4. F - This statement is a fact because you can always check the information with Mrs. Quinn.

D. ⇨

Lesson 2 (pages 70–73)

A. Fact: The national unemployment rate has fallen steadily for the last eighteen months, it rests at 5.2%, and the jobless rate is 30% for city youths.
Opinion: The writer feels that the jobless rate for city youth is one of our nation's most troubling social problems.

B. ⇨   C. ⇨   D. ⇨

E. 1. The right of teachers and school employees to strike
2. Everyone has the right to strike.
3. Teachers and other school officials do not have the right to strike if it interferes with the educational development of the nation's youth.

F. ⇨

Lesson 3 (pages 74–77)

A. ⇨   B. ⇨   C. ⇨

Lesson 4 (pages 78–79)

A. Answers will vary. Here are some samples:
1. tulip, rose, daffodil
2. milk, coffee, tea
3. broken bottles, old newspapers, potato peels
4. car, bus, subway
5. cancer, measles, chickenpox

B. Answers will vary. Here are some possibilities:
1. courthouse, store, apartment house
2. boom, bang
3. plumbers, dentists, police officers
4. at the Town Hall, at the Civic Center
5. institutions, homes, hospitals

C. Answers will vary. Here are some possibilities:
1. stroll, tread, saunter
2. chatter, prate, gab
3. gobble, chew, devour

D. Your answers may be similar to these:
1. stated, demanded
2. sauntered, strolled, shuffled
3. bolted or gulped his food, shouted or yelled
4. whispered

E. ⇨

Unit 6

Lesson 1 (pages 82–85)

A. Answers should be similar to these:
1. Oliver is a braggart.
2. Todd is conceited.
3. Penelope is a nag.
4. Helga is a pig.

B. 1. The writer thought the room was a mess and very depressing to be in.
2. cramped, messy, strewn, dumped, ancient, and bleak
3. negative

C. 1. For *messy* you might substitute *lived-in.*
2. For *strewn* you might substitute *displayed.*
3. For *dumped* you might substitute *piled neatly.*
4. For *ancient* you might substitute *antique.*
5. For *bleak* you might substitute *serene.*

D. a. You should have underlined: *perk up, new friends, talk of the town, Good Impressions, up-to-date.*
You should have circled: *lonely, out of touch, boring.*
b. You should have underlined: *Sunshine, float away, shining smile.* You should have circled: *rubs you the wrong way, despair, aches and pains.*
c. You should have underlined: *Slim-Trim, golden opportunity, latest, slick, stylish, chic, low prices, Slim and Trim, new.* There are no minus-words in the ad.

E. ⇨

Lesson 2 (pages 86–89)

A. 1. Possible answers are: the name of the book, the author, the main character, and the setting.
2. The reviewer says the book is a thriller about a young woman who is trying to find out where her visions come from.
3. The reviewer liked the book because it was well written and the main character was convincing.

4. The reviewer feels that the other characters did not stand out enough.

5. The reviewer recommends the book to other people by applauding the book and hoping another is on its way.

B. 1. The setting is a futuristic home. The characters are two people and two robots.

2. You may say it's about the future struggle between people and machines.

3. The audience is laughing and seems to be enjoying the play.

4. You would need to include your own opinion and the reasons for your views.

C. ➩ **D.** ➩

Lesson 3 (pages 90–93)

A. 1. business letter

2. Alexander saw a sign in the bake shop window.

3. He has helped out at home, he is a fast learner, he lives across the street from the shopping center and can always be at work on time, and he does not have a sweet tooth.

4. Alexander is asking to set up an appointment.

5. He told Ms. Seiden when he could meet with her and gave her his telephone number.

B. ➩ **C.** ➩

Lesson 4 (pages 94–95)

A. Here are some possible answers:

1. The memories of sun-filled days get me through the slush and the cold.

2. Although winter may have pleasures for some, I find myself concentrating on ways to keep warm and dry.

3. I like to curl up with a good book in front of a roaring fire.

4. My book forgotten, I dream of summer and finally feel warmth and contentment stealing over me.

B. Answers should be similar to this:

As Simone stepped off the plane, she was greeted by tall tropical plants and sweet-smelling air. From the airport, she could see the green mountains rising in the background. She couldn't wait to get to her room, unpack her bags, and take a long swim in the ocean. Simone felt so lucky to be home again, where she was the most comfortable. She had enjoyed her visit with her grandmother, but she wouldn't trade living on this island for anything!

Unit 7

Lesson 1 (pages 98–101)

A. ➩ **B.** ➩ **C.** ➩ **D.** ➩ **E.** ➩

Lesson 2 (pages 102–105)

A. TP 1. FP 2. FP 3. TP 4.

B. ➩ **C.** ➩ **D.** ➩ **E.** S 1. O 2.

F. ➩ **G.** ➩

Lesson 3 (pages 106–109)

A. ➩ **D.** ➩ **G.** ➩

B. ➩ **E.** ➩ **H.** ➩

C. ➩ **F.** ➩ **I.** ➩

Lesson 4 (pages 110–111)

A. Your answers may be similar to these:

1. In the ninth inning the batter hit the ball hard into the bleachers.

2. Shop for winter clothes now when spring clothes are already out. Since winter clothes are on clearance sale, you can get some real bargains.

3. On top of the old battered desk lay a worn-out brown diary which had two faded 50-year-old photographs inside.

4. The Coast Guard cutter approached the survivors who were desperately clinging to life rafts.
With the survivors wrapped in blankets to keep warm, the cutter headed into port.

5. Staying in the haunted house made Kerry feel as if he was going to jump out of his skin.

6. Everyone in the class will go to Jim's Halloween party tonight.

7. After breakfast, I get on my bicycle and ride north on long, winding country roads. I see woods and farms with red barns off in the distance.

B. Here is one possible revision:
The night was dark and chilly when Sarah heard a noise outside her window. Suddenly, a mysterious figure leapt into the bedroom. When Sarah screamed loudly, the bedroom door flew open. The police rushed in, and she was safe.

Writing Handbook (page 126)

A.   The most popular~~est~~ rodent in the world, _M_ickey _M_ouse, was born in 1928. He ~~maked~~ *made* his screen debut in <u>Steamboat Willie,</u> the first cartoon to use sound. Walt Disney, the man who ~~drawed~~ *drew* Mickey, also provided the mouse's voice. Since his first film was released, Mickey has made countless/other films and has bec*o*me world famous. Now Mickey's big ears, bow tie, and white gloves ~~is~~ *are* recognized everywhere. Can ~~their~~ *there* be anyone who ~~don't~~ *doesn't* know and love this mouse among ~~mouses~~ *mice?* *T*he ageless star now ~~have~~ *has* two homes. Disneyland in Anaheim, California, was opened on July 17, 1955, and Disney World in Orlando, *F*lorida, was opened in 1971.

128

Post-Test Answers; pg 16

1. a. C
    b. L
    c. C
    d. L
2. Outlines will vary. Students should include at least two main heads (Roman numerals) followed by subheads (capital letters). Sub-sub-heads should have arabic numbers.
3. Anecdotes will vary. The first sentences should refer to the present-time situation which leads into the "flashback" with transition words or sentences.
4. Answers may vary.
    a. The assembly <u>cheered</u> the president.
    b. Jean <u>scribbled</u> a note to her homeroom teacher.
    c. Tony <u>argued</u> with Denis over the best football team.

Post-Test Answers; pg 32

1. Wording mary vary slightly.
    a. People start panting during hard exercise because their bodies need more oxygen.
    b. The increased oxygen helps remove the lactic acid that is produced by the muscles.
2. Answers may vary slightly.
    Therefore, the thief must have been someone familiar with the house.
3. a. The whale nourishes its young with milk.
    b. Therefore this water sample is pure.
4. Paragraphs will vary. Students may begin with a cause topic sentence, such as *The discovery of fire changed history.* The rest of the paragraph may list effects of the discovery of fire.

Post-Test Answers; pg 48

1. b and d.
2. Paragraphs will vary. Make sure that the details chosen are appropriate to the mood the student wants to create.
3. Answers will vary. Possible answers:
    a. ...you can see the stars so clearly.
    b. ...the landscape is artificial.
4. Answers may vary slightly.
    a. In Congress, Senator Seal is the strongest champion of wildlife.
    b. From the hospital room, the exhausted sailor told an incredible tale of survival on a liferaft.

Post-Test Answers; pg 64

1. Answers may vary.
    a. Jamie's speech was a beacon that lit our course of action.
    b. Lana's voice was usually gentle, but sometimes it could cut like a knife.
    c. Detective Bunsen reminded me of a cheetah stalking its prey.
2. Possible answers:
    a. ...plunging from the high diving board.
    b. ...declaring war.
    c. like a week's groceries for most people.
3. Possible answers:
    a. The tennis ball kept returning like a boomerang.
    b. The subway train is a long, steel snake winding under the city.
    c. The tree was a dancer in a long rustling skirt.
4. Paragraphs will vary. The fable or parable can be a humorous, imaginative, or literal illustration of the moral.

Post-Test Answers; pg 80

1. a. N
   b. E
   c. N
   d. E
2. Answers will vary. Be sure that each opinion relates to the fact.
3. Speeches will vary. The best speeches will include specific qualifications and ideas, as well as facts to support them.
4. Possible answers:
   a. We spied a monkey hiding in a tree.
   c. The writer lectured on her childhood in Mississippi.

Post-Test Answers; pg 90

1. Answers will vary. Possible answers:
   a. Jeffery is so concerned about other people's affairs.
   b. Shawna always dresses casually.
2. Ads will vary. The best ads will use loaded words in imaginative, catchy ways.
3. Answers will vary. Some possible answers:
   a. babysitting experience
   b. good with figures
   c. take care of neighbors' yards
4. Students should mention two of the following: The author's name, reasons for the reviewer's opinion, and suggestions as to whether others will like the book are all missing.
5. Answers will vary slightly. Possible answer:
   After the concert started, Linda's violin string snapped. She had to go backstage to get a new string. The audience grew restless until Linda returned. Then the orchestra started from the beginning.

Post-Test Answers; pg 112

1. Paragraphs will vary. Students may write f from the point of view of a crew member, passenger, or airport employee.
2. The point of view is probably that of a biologist working in a zoo.
3. a. S
   b. O
4. Answers will vary. A possible answer:
   Since my parents were both in the army, they traveled a lot. I was born in France and my brother was born in Germany. Living different countries, we became familiar with other cultures. Although making new friends was sometimes difficult, it was an interesting life.